LETTER FROM A FATHER
Understanding Oneself

BLAZIO MZILAWEMPI

Written by Blazio Mzilawempi

Published by Hoart Benom (Pty) Ltd - Publishing
Cape Town, South Africa

Contributions:
Sinqobile Zilawe (BEd., MEd. Foundation Psychology);
Auxie Mzil-Lehang; Lebo Lebohang
Folklore: Auxie Mzil-Lehang; P. Utsiwegota Chirau (LLb)

To order books or for customer service, please email
oxy.lehang@gmail.com

ISBN 978-0-620-91330-0

Ebook 978-0-620-91331-7

Copyright © 2021 Hoart Benom (Pty) Ltd
All rights reserved. No part of this publication may be reproduced, stored in a retrieval system, or transmitted in any form by any means electronic, mechanical, photocopying, recording or otherwise without the written permission of the copyright owner.

This book is printed on acid-free paper ∞

TO

*Beauty, my wife and best friend of many decades.
There are no perfect words to describe how much I
appreciate you, just for being the special person you are*

*My late brother S. Mpala and his wife Nightingale.
I'm always grateful for the warmth and generosity
you showed me, especially in my days of trying. Heaven is
richer with you.*

*All my children.
You were the initial reason I penned this letter...*

AND

All readers of the book – my sincere gratitude!

CONTENTS

Preface	.. ..	7
Chapter I	Introduction: Understanding Oneself and Being In Good Functioning Order	9
Chapter II	How Confidence and Personality are Born ..	13
Chapter III	Controlling One's Thoughts..	23
Chapter IV	The Power to Command Attention	28
Chapter V	How to Go-On Being A Positive, ... Purposeful Personality..	40
Chapter VI	Character, Social Life And Ethics	43
Chapter VII	Confronting Challenges Head-On	54
Chapter VIII	Life of A Confident Adult Individual..	59
Chapter IX	How Not to Be Influenced By What .. .. Others Say Or Do	70
Chapter X	You're The Salesman Of Your Own Life	82
Chapter XI	Unpacking The Inability to Move Forward ..	87
Chapter XII	Information On General Health .. .. .. And Success in Job Seeking	99
Conclusion	.. ..	108
Epilogue	.. ..	109
Bibliography	.. ..	117

PREFACE

Growing up, I was exposed to the outside world at a tender age. My eyes opened up to the realities of life pretty early and I came to an understanding that we scarcely lived in the lap of luxury. My life then wasn't doom and gloom all the way; I always reached out whenever I felt my faculties were at stake. The path was, however, dotted with numerous challenges; some minute and others huge. I literally had to cross dangerous rivers for a couple of years in my quest to get an education. I was later taken in by a good-hearted older cousin who had identified my passion and tenacity and was facilitated into a great high school, where he had been placed as the principal. During his tenure, he adopted quite a number of other youngsters too, who were in a similar predicament. I am now a homeopath practitioner and involved in agribusiness today.

I'm just an ordinary father, like any other. I was born in 1950. My own father crossed over to the other side of the horizon in his forties. He had been enthroned as succeeding chief in part of Mashonaland, West Province in Zimbabwe, but did not rule for long. Not much was left for the family upon his passing. I stumbled over different kinds of hurdles as I propelled onwards with life. Young and staggeringly vulnerable, I had to hustle to make ends meet. I stayed positive, even though it was very hard sometimes. All the challenges I encountered then made me wonder if my children, in the future, would possibly have been able to stand on their own should I have not made it to watch them grow up.

My father's passing made me look at life from a different perspective, with amplified comprehension. I visualised then – given that days on earth are numbered – and I feared the possibility of my own children having to grow up without their father. I thought about being absent and unable to cheer them along and hold their hands whenever they felt like the world was crashing down on them. I then began penning this letter in my early adulthood. I felt it would be somewhat impactful, and perhaps I'd be able to help strengthen them and guide their paths, like a guardian would.

It was precisely fifty years before the publication date endorsed on the first official copy (2021) when I began with my research and heartfelt writing. I completed the manuscript a few years later. My first-born child had not been born yet and neither was I yet married! I knew children were to come one day; my intuition always whispered that to me. I was betrothed by the time I completed the project.

Now, seeing my children all grown and them being blessed with their own children – my grandchildren! – I felt it befitting to say yes to some requests that I share the letter on the world stage. So, I revised it, got it reviewed and here it is! LETTER FROM A FATHER… Understanding Oneself.

Hopefully, it helps to inspire somebody in some way or another. It may assist in the general upkeep of mental strength and staying resilient, regardless of the many different prevailing negative forces that roam around the world.

CHAPTER I

INTRODUCTION: UNDERSTANDING ONESELF AND BEING IN GOOD FUNCTIONING ORDER

Understanding oneself means gaining an in-depth perception of you as an individual, which is a great step towards achieving self-validation, and insulating your stature. If you understand yourself first, it makes it easier for you to understand other people better and you'll be in a position to relate to them more easily. Recognising your self-worth, which is 'self-validation', ignites the willpower, an essential tool in planning and setting goals, as well as in accomplishing them. The process also helps to restore, or ignite, strength; and thereby creates resilience that is very necessary to overcome challenges.

In general, life has challenges, and yes, they're bound to happen at some point... be they big or small. They spring forth in different forms and at different magnitudes. When appropriately handled, challenges and changes add zest and sparkle to life. They are supposed to stir-up one's imagination – thus enabling an individual to embark on a different mind journey of methodical formulation of ideas – and strategically executing them. The latter is enabled through the natural power of 'adaptive energy', which is derived from within; and is substantially strengthened by constant self-contemplation sessions, amongst other ways.

Adaptive energy is the flow of energy needed to help nourish the mind in times of stress or adversity. If personal response to some definite situation stays rigid, it risks choking up the beautiful flow of adaptive energy, thereby robbing the mind of its natural ability to conquer stress. It might become hard to project a positive outcome in such a scenario. There is a likelihood, too, of failing to construct great solutions to solve particular problems. The Oxford Dictionary describes adaptive energy as the hypothetical measure of an individual's capacity to resist stress.

Introspection or thoughtfulness need to be in good functional order for you to be able to respond to stressful situations in a balanced way. If equilibrium suffers, one side might be left bruised – you either become sick or make a regrettable move. Healthy decision making is better done, and far more effective, when you understand yourself. Famous psychoanalysis theorist Sigmund Freud once gave a great way of understanding yourself by saying, "Turn your eyes inward, and look into your own depths; learn to first know yourself." If you are perceptive of yourself, a burst of adaptive energy can move freely and will support sufficient creativity of the mind to glide on.

Should you, however, feel very pressured in the mind – like the walls are crushing in on you – and you are failing to cope with whatever challenges you are facing, do not be ashamed to seek help. There is a wide range of other factors that might drain or block the adaptive energy reservoirs. Almost everybody goes through a rough patch at some point. Even the most successful individuals reach out at some point.

With the world having gone through outbreaks of war, natural disasters and pandemics, the question of human behaviour has now attracted more attention than perhaps in previous times. Some people's personal problems have somewhat increased beyond conception, emanating from different angles. Consequently, their attitude and approach to life could have visibly changed, and so may their needs and interests. Mind treatment has meanwhile increased in proportion to demand. Many books have been written and more therapeutic institutions formed to cater for both mind and general health, to try and meet with man's needs. Man has become more aware of himself – not only as far as introspection goes, but intelligence too has increased.

Good support from either close friends or relatives can be crucial in times of adversity. It surely relieves strain and gives comfort too, as well as hope and a sense of wellbeing. Should there be no reliable person/s within your immediate circle or surroundings to sit down with, seeking professional advice or help is a good idea. Medical help, psychological help or counselling institutions are generally available. There's absolutely no need to feel ashamed of what might be revealed.

That way, you'll learn how to gain or enhance your strength and will be able to revive and cultivate from the positivity that lies inside of you. If all goes well, you'll then be able to move on with life strategically, with much improved confidence. Psychological science embodies an ideal healthy living lifestyle. Good health is of paramount importance to a sound and productive life. Self-help books and counselling also promote this. They teach about human behaviour and they also aim at destroying the germs of anxiety and microbes of fear even before they begin to exponentially grow, spreading in all directions through the mental frame of the human body. Nervous anticipation can be destroyed, as well as unnecessary apprehension and negative suggestions – all being replaced with hopeful expectation.

The work of a psychologist, or the theories put across, are not to make you see those individuals' way of life, but to see your own, revealed by the laying bare of the x-ray negative of your mind. In step with the man's forward march, psychological help is progressing as the years go by. The mind of an average person is different today from what it was, say, three decades ago. New conflicts have risen in-between. New treatments are thence necessitated to meet up with sprouting drawbacks. Cure lies in the state that is completely conscious and self-determined.

Psychological succour can help you to sustain yourself when you feel you can't handle some circumstances all by yourself. It lays down certain tenets and laws to counter the problem. Thereafter, it is up to the individual's effort. Thus, great self-introspection is very important. It supports an individual to be able to exercise a reasonable control over the conscious mind, thus permitting the subconscious to fall into the correct perspective.

Introspection, when applied rationally, can give us new directions to manoeuvre around obstacles. It also unveils any faults or mistakes, should there be any, that might need to be corrected for us to confidently move forward and realise our dreams. So, introspection or personal analysis and diagnosis can assist an individual to help themselves in navigating and gathering knowledge that may assist not just them, but help in protecting others as well, within their spaces of daily living. It bestows level-headedness. It's good to also keep in mind that reflection on successes gives inner peace too and should boost your confidence, thus enabling you to spur on to next levels.

CHAPTER II

HOW CONFIDENCE AND PERSONALITY ARE BORN

The very first cry a new-born child utters could be considered as evidence of its personality. It is the very first protest against life's challenges. The baby now has to breathe on its own, complain when hungry or not comfortable as well as signal those moments when not feeling well. It is magnificent at the same time, to be born; a chance to be a part of the universe. A mother will know eventually the particular cry for milk, or that one for diaper change, and the call of tiredness when the baby wants to nap. As the child grows, the parents watch its little habits grow too. The way it smiles, or the way it laughs and cries... all scenarios are registered in memory by the parents – including all the ways that the offspring fights to get what it wants.

NOW IS BORN CONFIDENCE...
Every child has its own individuality, unspoiled so far by people and other influences. The child is unafraid because it does not yet know the meaning of fear. It expresses itself in the way it absolutely feels – carefree, up to perhaps the time it goes to school. Before then, its personality development will still be controlled by home life. This is where the first impact of the environment on the individual starts; in the home. As children grow, they learn unconsciously and suck up almost everything presented or exposed to them along the way. This stage of growing up is one of the most crucial programming stages of

their lives. Some have referred to it as the 'monkey see – monkey do' phase.

Given an average home life, all will be good, but with the approach of school days, personality undergoes great change. Confidence is severely shaken. The child's mind and eyes are opened to the unpleasantness that exists beyond the safety and security of the home or nursery. Personality traits develop and, if allowed, they reign fully as nurtured by the parents and encouraged by relatives and friends. The traits get engrained in the child's subconscious mind.

Media content that's fed into the public domain may have a great influence on children too, in either positive or negative ways. It is the nature of content that determines its impact in relation to a child's age. It is therefore a huge responsibility on the adult in charge to ensure appropriateness of what a child's mind consumes at any given time. Children should not be subjected to things that will force their minds into growing up more quickly, thereby being deprived of the privilege of just being kids. They ought to enjoy their childhood in peace and to the fullest without being driven into anxiety-triggering issues of an adult nature.

As they go to school, new impressions arise, new faces confront the child, and the world grows visibly larger and might seem or become minacious to the young minds. Teachers take over in many ways to supplant parents. From these school-age days will spring forth the personality potential and the confidence that sets the child's pattern of life. Many qualities may fight for first place in the child's growing mind. These qualities also arise from interaction with the world. Children are like sponges: they can easily absorb what surrounds them. There's no one as sensitive, as true or genuine and unspoiled, as a child who has not learned about life. Children are precious and need to be protected against evil.

The process of growing could be sad. Being born is enough of a shake up – leaving the soothing comfort and absolute safety of a mother's womb, to be faced with the inevitable task of growing daily; bigger in the mind and body, further and further away from the sanctity of the womb... going nearer and nearer to the harshness and deceptions of life is mental and physical experience that could be beset with anguish.

PERSONALITY

Personality refers to the unique internal and external relatively enduring aspects that influence an individual's behaviour when faced with different situations (Schultz & Schultz, 2011).

Personality is the general characterisation,
Or pattern of an individual's total behaviour.
Aggregate sum of your demeanour ascribes to personality.
It is the coherent aura that surrounds an individual:
The shimmer of vibrations emanating from within a person –
And outer, the vibrations vacillate like magnetic flux – widening in laps;
Rubbing off to all and everything with which they come into contact.
Personality is the touch of life;
Its magnificence, its symphony and its belongingness, or otherwise.
Personality is an appreciation of beautiful things too
It is beauty in itself!
Personality is 'You'
You carry personality wherever you are.

It is relatively stable even when you try to hide,
Or mask its traits;
Bubbly, affectionate, enthusiastic, frosty...
A hint flicks!
Personality finds a path of revealing itself always...
There's no hue that's entirely deficient of chromaticity;
Thus personality,
Bright yellow to crimson red
It is 'identity'

Personality development goes through many stages before it takes final shape and form. The traits are usually fully determined in semi-adult and adult life. Theories of Gordon Allport, one of the earliest great psychologists, postulate that traits refer to what is peculiar to an individual. Thus, during that period of life, the behaviour of a particular individual may show, for example, whether or not they are introverts or extroverts. Personality will have developed.

It can be a far cry in life from that first cry made upon entering the world, when born. However, with proven facts that man develops a degree of confidence that builds up to personality, it eventually emerges as an indisputable fact whether his personality makes a great impression on life, whether the degree of his confidence is enough to fight life's battles; all dependant on an individual's circumstances and personal encounters – as we grow older each day. Some factors, a deterrent or threat to one's confidence, will be discussed as we delve further into the book. Ways to galvanize, insulate and as well raise one's degree of resistance to obstacles will be covered too.

The personality of an individual may be affected by interactions with others. According to Humanists, people who develop a positive personality are those who have grown up in an environment that offers unconditional positive regard (Rogers in Dwairy, 2002). Thus, if an individual grows up in an accepting, encouraging and persuasive environment, a pleasing personality and identity develops. Erik Erikson (1902-1994) argues that, if during the stage of identity versus identity confusion an individual fails to develop identity, they have an identity crisis. The identity crisis also has a negative impact on an individual's personality and confidence as they develop into an adult. Therefore, it's imperative to understand how the human mind generally operates.

GENERAL MECHANISM OF MIND

The human brain consists of three principal parts: forebrain with cerebrum, which forms the largest part of the brain and from which we get retention of memories and our intelligence. Then there's the midbrain for motor movement and visual processing. The third part is the hindbrain. This is mainly the cerebellum and brain stem. The brain stem is situated right at the beginning of the spinal cord. This part connects the brain to the spinal cord. It is composed of the pons and the medulla oblongata. The brain stem is vital in coordinating heartbeat, breathing, blood pressure and digestion – as well as reflexes like coughing, sneezing and swallowing. Finally, the 'sort of little brain image' cerebellum is at the extreme back; this section assists with our balance. See Figure 1 on the next page.

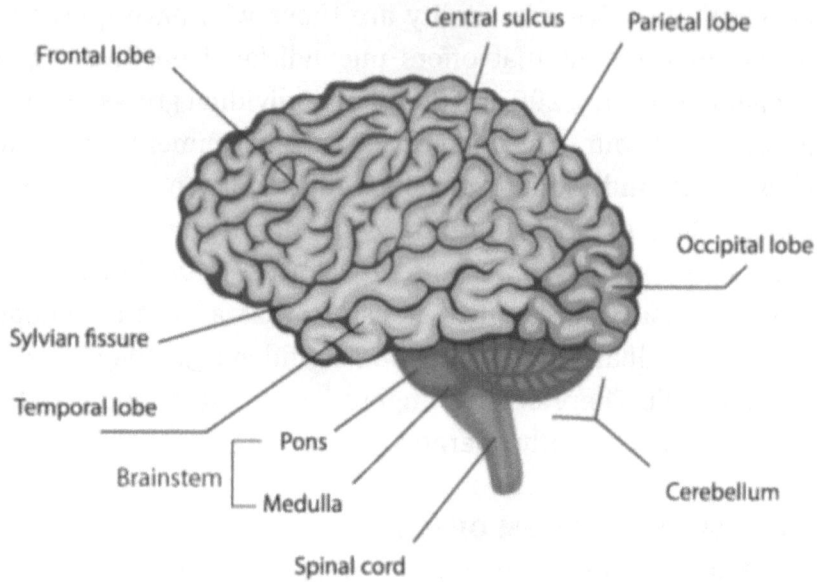

Figure 1: The Brain

The brain and the spinal cord have a protective covering of three membranes, and these are called maters. The outer layer is thick, the middle consists of small blood vessels and the inner covering enwraps the brain and spinal cord. Basically, the left side of the brain controls the right side of the body. The right side of the brain controls the left side of the body. This is so because the nerves cross before going into the brain from the spinal cord.

On the cerebrum surface, 'a factory of vitality' houses the following:

- *Frontal lobe* – this part is responsible for self-awareness, emotions, personality, cognitive skills, problem solving and behavioural patterns, amongst other functions.
- *Parietal lobe* – is mainly responsible for sensing actions such as touch, temperature and pain. It interprets language as well as signals from vision and hearing. It also processes memory.
- *Occipital lobe* – this part interprets colour and movement, and helps with vision interpretation.
- *Temporal lobe* – this part is responsible for hearing, sequencing, memory, taste, understanding language and speech synthesis.

Memories comprise of short-term memory, long-term memory, and skill memory; and they are stored and involved in different parts of the brain. The processes involve encoding, storing and recalling.

Some diseases are only synthesised in the brain but can subsequently shift and start having effects onto the body.

Conversion Neurosis

A neurosis is a disorder of the nervous system for which no lesion change in organs or injury to any part of the body is present or found (Maldonado & Spiegel, 2001). That means no organic physical explanation is present and it is therefore of the mind.

In some cases, however, it can be partially or aggressively physical – that's becoming conversion neurosis. A conversion neurosis is the shifting of worry or mental anguish to a physical disability. It escapes from mental distress and moves to other parts of the body, for example, paralysis of a limb, cessation of the faculty of seeing, inability to easily swallow food, phantom pregnancy and the like. An individual converts his mental strain to a bodily illness. This could be a form of *defence mechanism:* some physical disability brought about by a desire to mask something or mitigate an encounter perceived by the mind as fearful or undesirable.

DEFENCE MECHANISMS

These are strategies used to defend oneself against anxiety and involve distorting or denying reality (Bowins, 2004). It could also be argued that there are times when they are necessary, as they may aid in maintaining emotional balance. However, more often than not, defence mechanisms are used as a scapegoat. In some cases, illness is used not as an escape but as a defence against unwanted action – "I am ill, so I cannot do ABC..." – but that loss of your voice before a scheduled public appearance may be very frustrating in some instances. The loss of voice is a result of fear, which will be in the sub-conscious mind. It could be on grounds of feeling intimidated and might manifest itself in the loss of voice. Thus, defence mechanisms may be revived from the sub-conscious, which is the core here. Defence Mechanisms can work in your favour or against, depending on your circumstances.

THE INFLUENCE OF DEFENCE MECHANISMS

When an individual is feeling emotionally unwell, defence mechanisms may be deployed. It creates a positive or negative effect upon a person and towards the body part in target. Illness can also be brought about by constant concentration upon a part or parts of our body. Blood can be rushed to that spot, nerve or tissues and they might get inflamed – thereby causing pain to set in. Nervous tension is increased, and the pain can intensify further. That is the mechanism of the illness wished upon oneself. Below are some cases of the defence mechanisms applied by people.

Infantile Regression

Regression is a defence mechanism in which an individual retreats to an earlier period of life that was less frustrating (Bowins, 2004). Thus, infantile regression involves a subconscious action of an individual going back in their mind to a period of their childhood where they were not threatened and felt very secure; that time when warmth, protection, freedom from responsibility were most apparent and pleasing. The individual may end up behaving childishly. A person may tell themselves, "I am ill," as a way of trying to find comfort and may even start sucking their thumb. Another classic trait is of a grown man or woman who returns to their mother every time he or she feels ill. Pouting, sulking, bad temper – all these moods in an adult could indicate subconscious return to childhood.

Compensation

Compensation arises from wanting to make up for failures in one area by excelling in another. It sometimes happens too when trying to make up for some specific injuries of the past, be it emotional or physical.

In 2015, part of my left arm got injured very badly. I fell whilst trying to run away in haste when I came face to face with a retaliating snake, so unexpectedly, in my residential yard. I dislocated my wrist. It was a terrible incident – although the snake didn't strike me in the end. It escaped in the opposite direction, probably startled by my loud screams and the shattering spectacles when I fell. It took me a long while before I fully recuperated, and that was almost two years. At one point the doctors had thought to remove part of the arm because of severely damaged nerves. Luckily, that never happened and I eventually recovered, but only after rigorous procedures. Tell you what? After that I doubled my farming area, compensating for the once-lost freedom of doing work and in celebration of an arm that had come to the verge of being lost! Funnily, I never calculated for it; it just happened subconsciously, but I was able to pick it up through retrospective introspection.

Imagined Bodily Complaints
"Each day I have vague pains round the region of my heart, but my doctor says there is nothing wrong." Well, the doctor might be right in saying so, and your health could be in a perfectly sound condition. Since you focus so much attention on your heart, the breathing processes of your body work overtime, in tune with your anxiety about yourself. This causes the amount of blood with which your heart deals to be out of proportion to its capacity. Each organ of the body has a faculty of its own governing it – controlled by the brain, which is ready to react in either a positive or negative manner depending on the impressions and suggestions relayed to it.

CHAPTER III

CONTROLLING ONE'S THOUGHTS

Self-talk can have an impact on self-worth. It can bring about negativity as much as it can inspire positivity. Thus, the mind needs to be controlled. It is the power of auto suggestion, which is also discussed in other topics. What we say to ourselves will either nurture or break us apart. Below are scenarios where an individual might be able to control their thoughts to change for the better.

Nerves
"I am a bundle of nerves; I never seem calm or poised. What can I do?" Relax, lie on your back on the bed and close your eyes. Let your body become fluid from the tips of your toes to your head. Decree a golden pass to your muscles and your nerves – to float in space, whimsically. Feel the soothing effect of letting yourself go. Then redeem yourself mentally. Dismiss all worrisome thoughts. Make your mind blank. Relaxation is a natural secret weapon for controlling nerves. What you are doing is letting the bundle loosen up. Have a cup of warm water afterwards, or soothing tea.

Sea Sickness or Motion Sickness
"Being on water makes me sick. As soon as I am on board, even before the ship launches, my stomach churns." But is this natural? This is far from being natural, but can turn out very badly. It cannot be viewed as being ludicrous. The swirl of a ship upsets the balancing fluid in the ear transmitting the messages

to the brain; then in turn sends it back to the stomach, causing the revolt of that organ as a defence reaction. When the ship or boat has not even begun to move, the balancing mechanism is in perfect order. All feelings of sickness come mainly from the mind. It is possible by the control of thought to so balance or imbalance your physical self! In this instance, there could be absolute power to overcome seasickness completely – even in heavy seas. The same applies to other scenarios of motion sickness like ski sickness, carsickness, elevator sickness and escalator sickness. Always try and incline toward positivity.

Obsessions

"I find it very hard to go to bed before I check all the gas taps and stove knobs two or three times, and before I've made sure that the front and back doors are locked." You know perfectly well that you have turned the gas off and switched off your stove, and that the doors are locked. What you doubt is that these physical movements in your part of the body are effective. You could be simply obsessed. Obsessions are unwanted persistent urges that an individual finds difficult to control despite many attempts (Clark & Gonzalez, 2014).

Sleeplessness Problem

"Going to sleep is really a nightmare to me. My mind never settles down, although I have active days; I lie awake at night and it seems that sleep deserts me as soon as I put my head on the pillow. The doctor tells me there is nothing wrong with me." Well, it is an unfortunate thing that the mind can force the body to forget how fatigued it is. As soon as your head touches the pillow your body receives messages from your mind to immediately start thinking. Your mind starts going around and round. When this happens, you have the power to avoid it under normal circumstances. If you start counting sheep, fight it immediately. Getting a good sleep is very important. It revitalises the body. It solidifies memory too, boosting creativity and willpower, amongst many other things. Early to bed, early to rise, makes a man healthy, wealthy and wise.

Anxiety

Anxiety comes as a response to stress. Everything we do in life can be overshadowed by acute anxiety and this is invariably followed by long fits, depression, loss of confidence in oneself and so on. You cannot help but become anxious about literally everything. If you are anxious, you overtax your mental output, and might end up in depression. You can do away with anxiety through having much more to look forward to, and that requires the 'plus energy' of positive thinking.

SELF-THERAPY AFFIRMATIONS AS CONFIDENCE BUILDERS

a. **Against Stomach Troubles or Similar**

This is today; your stomach is perfectly fit. Now, tell your stomach so.
"I have never felt better in my life. My stomach is clean and pure. It is strong, and will resist any trouble with which I have to contend. I am eating all the right foods, and doing all the righteous things. It is good to feel so well! No worry will ever upset my stomach... Since my stomach is so fit, I have no worries. Should any worries grow, well, I possess such a strong stomach to help me overcome them."

b. **Against Lack of Confidence**

"I am aware of my responsibilities. I have the courage and the capabilities to face them. There is nothing that cannot be solved. I am a tower of strength. I am capable. I am strong in the mind and body. I can make my own decisions, control my affairs, and I fear nothing!!"

c. **Against Confused Thinking**

"I have a crystal clear mind. I can absorb all thoughtful points and I'm able to retain all of them. I can bring the thoughts into immediate action and apply them wherever there's need and whenever there's a chance or opportunity for the betterment of anything. I have great power of concentration. Nothing will escape my agile mind. I am affirmative – steady in thinking and I'm in full possession of my thinking capacity."

d. **Suggestion**

Suggestion is the most powerful force in our lives. It could be auto-suggestion – emanating from inner self, or hetero-suggestion – emanating from outside. The subject is detailed in other parts of the book. There cannot possibly be life without suggestion. It is the direction behind every action, thought, word and deed – and this goes for everyone.

There is a state of mind called the 'death wish'. This is a compulsive desire to die. It can be born of hopelessness or fear of failure, amongst several other issues. Suicidal thoughts might come to the fore.

Keep in mind that there is a 'life wish' too – positive suggestion to drive towards prosperous living! Allow your mind to gravitate towards constructive energy. Set yourself onto a firm position to resist dwelling on negative thoughts, at any given time. Find a healthy escape whenever you feel overwhelmed. Powerful and inspiring music is always being created and released. Great and fun books are being written. More places of amusement have been – and are still being – invented. Explore. The world has so much to offer! Many people love life, so surround yourself with such characters. Wishful thinking is not enough. 'I wish' is merely a fantasy going around in the mind without any concrete action being taken to bring it out of the wish stage to life. Take charge, discover, and chronicle delightful stories!

CHAPTER IV

THE POWER TO COMMAND ATTENTION

Having a desire to earn something and then taking action to reach fruition can be counted as one of life's greatest gifts. A child has the power to command attention when they need something, and this may or may not be nurtured. The responses that the child gets after seeking attention may have an impact on building confidence and personality too. This brings about the impact of the environment an individual grows in.

Confidence of an individual can be influenced by self-esteem or self-efficacy, both of which result from interactions. Self-esteem is the feeling of self-worth and self-value, whilst self-efficacy is the belief that you can succeed in any area if you work hard (Hamza & Sahayaraj in Johnson, 2010). This implies that a combination of these two results in self-confidence, whilst lacking in one of them might result in an individual developing some hint of low self-confidence.

This brings us to the next section where we need to delve a little deeper, and perhaps discover whether you're perfectly fine – with self-esteem sitting at the right levels! Or you perhaps unmotivated in one area or another, or somewhat falling short of self-esteem. It could be caused by a feeling of inferiority or fear, amongst various other things. This should not be confused with being reserved, which is generally being calm, composed, conscientious and emotionally steady. Reserved characters have attributes of level-headedness, diplomacy and the like.

They are basically quiet, but can still be happy, confident and content.

WHAT IS INFERIORITY?

Inferiority is a state of feeling in self-esteem which results in negative self-evaluation (Neckel, 1996). Thus, inferiority is the state of mind – attitude of mind. Inferiority breeds a lack of confidence in oneself and consequently a lack of confidence in others. It robes one of one's self-assurance to speak well or more correctly and might even steal one's ambition. If it fails to get corrected, it can possibly affect one's life entirely, making one not fulfil one's most important goals – thus incapacitating all of one's prospects. Everyone has the right to live, and not just live well, but have sound well-being too.

No one is born with an inferiority complex; it is acquired through environmental circumstances and outside negative suggestions. Every man or woman has the right to be someone. Having a feeling of inferiority may result in the development of aggressive behaviour. Aggression can be founded on insecurity and lack of conviction. It is the cover-up for inadequacy. Inadequacy is mostly born of fear, and fear comes from insecurity. The sense of insecurity can be really frustrating to some individuals.

Inferiority is at the bottom of nearly every individual's troubles in the nuclear age. Inferiority arises from mistrust of oneself, others, circumstances and/or other things. The inferiority output of an average human being can be far more than the facts confronting him. When inferior feelings get out of hand, the cause can possibly grow to alarming proportions. The conditions get steadily worse, until a whole host of totally unnecessary complications arise – ones that would otherwise have not existed in the first place. It may however result in the development of an inferiority complex. It is possible, however, for a person to put a brake on his inferior feelings if he realises that he suffers from an inferiority complex and its attendant ills.

Do You Perhaps Feel Unmotivated?

You can ask yourself, am I at all inferior or do I just have a complex? A complex is a loosely used term usually associated with inferiority. A complex is a repressed group of forgotten ideas and impressions to which are ascribed abnormal bodily conditions due to mental causes that have been suppressed. An inferiority complex is having feelings of inferiority in relation to other individuals and may manifest itself through experiencing feelings of jealousy (Spearman, 2014). But, when you tell a friend that he could have an inferiority complex, it might be literally taken as meaning that they're cuckoo, which is not the case.

When one feels inferior, one may not want to mix with others; one might be afraid to face life and just find it so easy to tell oneself that the best way out is to simply shut down or stay low. That way, no one may feel confident enough to give you responsibility or authority. You will be able to go your own way, hiding deep down in your own made shell, running away from life and all that it has to offer.

If you feel like something could be holding you back, or you know that you suffer some degree of inferiority, do an introspection: do you feel inferior because you just want to be that way OR do you do feel inferior, but do not want to be? If you're certain that you have a feel of inferiority and surely need a change, just continue reading the book. Some aspects also encompass the matter.

WORD ASSOCIATION TEST TO ESTABLISH WHY YOU LACK CONFIDENCE

Here is something for reflection. It's a great sample of a Word Association Test carried out by psychologists by giving patients certain words and finding out their reaction towards them. It can possibly channel to the root cause of certain troubles and problems. As soon as a word, or set of words, or sequence of words, is spoken by the practitioner, certain immediate responses by the patient call a halt. What would you feel with the following words in Table 1 below? Be honest; you might possibly be able to identify where your problem lies and seek out how you might possibly break the mould to build your confidence. If you're positive throughout, then *bingo!* it should simply brace up your assurance to spur on.

Table 1: Word Association Test

Burglary	Red	Food	Stay
Wed	Light	Start	Flop
Pandemic	Catch	Thirst	Age
Quarrels	Meat	Virus	Fate
Life	Poor	Adult	Speak
Short	Bush	Moon	Table
Legs	Walk	Pen	Flowers
Mend	Sorrow	Joy	Sister
Husband	Purple	Ill will	Strong
Enemy	Travelling	Divorce	Halt

Weight	Bury	House	Seat
Ask	Spices	Nasty	Anxiety
Warm	Social media	Fresh	Party
Track	Habit	Flight	Lonely
Dance	Prayer	Confined	Brother
Town	Cash	Small	Clothes
Pool	Wise	Lose	Bewitched
Sick	Paper	Get	Weak
Vanity	Hate	Medication	Sorry
Take	Run	Cold	Miserable
Wife	Dull	Dark	Open
Peaceful	Boring	Spring	Hurt
Needles	Work	Case	Good
Sink	Family	Debt	Longing
Crowd	Inaccessible	Parents	Injury

If words such as ill-will, sink, dull, hate, sorrow, poor, nasty, hurt, miserable, sorry, confined or fate, amongst other negative words, frequent your vocabulary or make you very uneasy after reading them, it could be a sign that you have low self-confidence in something, or a particular incident that happened to you in the past could be really affecting you internally. That might certainly require some professional therapy to resolve – or you could speak to someone reliable in your circle. Another test like the one below can also be applied to help assess self-esteem.

Self-Report Inventory on Assessing Self-Esteem

Answer the following questions in Table 2 below to ascertain your level of self-esteem and ethics.

Table 2: Assessing Self Esteem

Do I get upset whenever things go wrong?	Do I act out when things don't go my way, by making others feel like I'm superior?
Do I dismiss things I do not comprehend?	When my wife/husband or lover admires another man/woman, do I get jealous or not?
Do I react by doing something active when I am frustrated?	
Do I feel unhappy when I am not interested in something or someone?	Do I easily feel hurt?
	Do I study/compare myself with others?
Do I like myself in a mirror?	
Do I have frequent quarrels with my relatives?	Do I get heartsick when my hopes are rejected?
Do I find it easy to admit when I am wrong?	Do I belittle competitors?
	Do I allow room for sensitive people with ease?
Do I adjust easily?	
Do I spend to impress people?	Do I dress or behave in a particular way just to attract attention?
Do I evade the results of my mistakes?	Do I allow my ears to listen to opinions of others?
Do I wonder what others think of me?	Do I feel life has dealt badly with me?
Do I always go with the crowd?	Do I want to exploit myself?
Do I allow past trivial issues to upset me?	Do I sense general depression?
Do I try to keep up appearances?	Do I keep my head cool in trouble?
	Do I blame others for my slow progress?

If most of the answers to the above questions are NEGATIVE, then you might be experiencing low self-esteem or overriding moral principles, which need to be repaired or discarded in order to develop a positive and pleasing character, as well as a bright personality. You need to equip yourself or reclaim the strength and capacity to assess situations or circumstances skilfully and be able to draw sound conclusions that benefit you and those around you.

Routine for Developing a Positive Pleasing Persuasive Personality – *for promoting poise and pose*

Below are some of the statements an individual needs to say to in order to develop a positive pleasing personality:

- I will smile and mean it. I'll feel the brightness right in my core.
- I will speak in pleasant, positive tones and be sincere.
- I will watch how I dress always; I'll be clean and well groomed.
- I will study the way I sit, stand, walk and use my hands.
- I will move with decision and know where I am going.
- I will think one thing at a time and will not let my thoughts wander about.
- I will always remember and respect that my brain should think one thing at a time so that I can come up with best solutions.

POWERFUL POSITIVE WORDS

To appropriately develop confidence, the following words, or similar, need to be part and parcel of your daily vocabulary:

Success	Ability	Action	Progress
Perspicacity	Appropriate	Initiative	Adaptability
Adjustment	Acceptance	Perseverance	Determination

Uplifting Words

Table 3: Uplifting Words

Free	Joyous	Bright	Hopeful	Victorious

I Words

Table 4: I Words

I will	I must
I can	I would
I shall	I'm able
I did	I should

Take the following words into your mind and safe keep them right inside, to build a foundation of a potentially great personality. Remember, memory and retention are followed by recall and thus the power or ability to remember.

- ✪ You assimilate → *take into mind.*
- ✪ You reflect → *mentally masticate and absorb.*
- ✪ You accept → *mentally digest.*
- ✪ You adapt → *turn situation into favour, to benefit yourself.*
- ✪ You apply → *use knowledge to the best possible advantage to prosper.*

Without disregarding any religious beliefs, life is simply thrust upon an individual without the asking. It is the result of a biological act between two people who so happen to become parents... You deserve a chance, like everyone else does too; a chance to live your life to the fullest and an equal opportunity! You are a person the moment you enter the world, and as a child the world is yours. You know no fears, for you have no reason to fear, as was discussed earlier. Allow the cognition to prevail into adulthood and never limit yourself intentionally – or unintentionally!

OUTWARD SIGNS OF CONFIDENCE

When I do not have these, I must make sure I cultivate them.

i. *Personal magnetism*, which is an off shoot of personality.
ii. A *well-dressed appearance,* which is clean and allows you to stand or move around with ease in your natural posture.
iii. A *cultured voice*, which shows you are well bred and know exactly what you want out of life.
iv. *Good manners*, which are an essential tool to gain confidence of friends, and business and social acquaintances. Manners make a man, but a man can also make manners.

PEOPLE WILL LOOK TO YOU

If they are to have confidence in you for:

i. *Your ability as a good listener* – you are a good listener if people are willing to tell you all, or when people confide in you and perhaps ask your advice or views to solve some issues.

ii. *Your ideals and principles* – these are born of your philosophy of life.
iii. *Your open mindedness* – and thus your sense of fair play. It is also your ability to some extent, not to judge fellow human and treat everyone as innocent until proven guilty.
iv. *Your ability to pass judgement* – only when the point has been well considered, not through hasty actions. Some decisions arouse suspicion too in some cases.

Confidence All Round You

To be able to contribute or make a positive impact in the world, you need to have a clear understanding of what is happening in your surroundings and perhaps beyond. Every moment of every day, imaginative individuals will be busy planning and designing new ways of getting things done:

- To invent new ways and means of making life more pleasant and enjoyable.
- Making new and healthier food products to eat and drink.
- Creating new fashion lines; fancier and more comfortable clothes to wear. More and more durable and longer lasting materials are emerging as well as recyclable/earth friendly products.
- New textiles to make homes brighter and more pleasant to live in are being manufactured.
- New models of transport to get you from here to there have increased. They're now quicker and are becoming more and more appealing.
- New ways of watching better and brighter television are being invented. We have louder and clearer sets nowadays,

with a wider range of options of what to watch at any given time than in the past.
- Recyclable materials are becoming more and more prominent in the production sector, to save and protect the environment.
- On the other hand, different kinds of warfare have also been made, with some being controversial on various platforms in the world. These are all designs created by the human mind. At the same time, surveillances are also becoming more and more sophisticated and effective to protect civilians.

All these examples are end results of confidence in inventions. Most of them, like many others being executed out there, are constructive, creative and progressive. Sift the good from the bad and underline what will be left to benefit humanity.

Now, Ask Yourself:
What am I doing that is of benefit to humanity? What do you do to give mankind confidence in you? What products of your brain contribute towards happier living?

We all cannot create something that will be of impact to the entire world at large, but at least we can contribute what we can in our capacity. If you can be of help to at least one person at a given time, that's already positive impact to the world. Strengths do not only end at talent or earned skills; character counts greatly too: social intelligence, general wisdom and knowledge... *to name a few*. We can contribute something to our immediate social, domestic and industrial spheres. This may be accomplished by applying all we can for the betterment of others, like being sociable, honest and industrious. It benefits us in turn too, in one way or another.

If someone wants to be nothing there is plenty of room for them still – wallowing in mental idleness. Some who could have been able to lead might be led instead, and those who might have been capable of caring might find themselves being the ones taken care of. You could be sitting on great potential that could be of influence/beneficial to other people, but just haven't realised it yet, or you simply suffocate the urge to start whenever you feel like bouncing forward. Go ahead: aspire and become the best possible version of yourself!

> *"One can never consent to crawl when one feels an impulse to soar"* – HELEN KELLER.

CHAPTER V

HOW TO GO-ON BEING A POSITIVE, PURPOSEFUL PERSONALITY

When the day is done, ask yourself if all went well on your way from the day's work. How have you treated the world in which you move? Were you bad tempered with the conductor, or with your car, if it did not start right away as you anticipated? Or with the chauffeur, if you felt that he drove somewhat too slow? Did you give everyone at the office or at your work place a good morning? How many positive thoughts did you project to those around you?

A Day in the Life of a Contented, Confident, Well-Balanced Person

He rises-up just before the alarm goes off because he has told his subconscious mind the night before the precise hour at which he has to wake up. The presence of the set alarm clock is to give him the added assurance that, should his subconscious let him down, all will still be well. This subconscious does not let him down, for he has trained it to obey his conscious well. Therefore, he wakes up just before the alarm goes off. He dresses quickly after washing and moisturising. A complete bath is always good if possible; it is freshening and rejuvenating to the mind and body, and that as well initiates a positive tone to the new day. He then breakfasts sensibly – cereals, tea, whole meal bread and butter, and he leaves home happy, with no shadows of what happened yesterday or previous night – for this is a completely new day.

Morning Reflections

I wish to make today better than yesterday. I must grasp every opportunity that comes my way. Nothing except getting nearer to perfection will satisfy my day today. Yesterday ended up in futility, but today is a different day. Now I am awake, I will command my actions from this moment on. I will assert myself without being overbearing. When today has ended, people will say oh! what a fine fellow, what a pleasant personality. That fellow knows what he wants and how to get it; he knows how to get things done... When I return from work, I'll will say I have done everything perfectly well – and when I go to sleep, I'll have had one of my finest days.

When you wake up in the morning, promise yourself to put right all the mistakes you may have made the previous day. Think carefully, and bear faith that you'll have a more pleasant day than yesterday. Mention the mistakes you made and how to improve or rectify them: "I will not be too quick with money today." "I will consider my words before I speak today."

Take a Long, Thoughtful Moment

My body and my mind need to obey me, for they are on my pay roll. I must treat them with respect, but I must not over-tax them either. I must nourish them well and rest them up at regular intervals, so that I don't get frustrated unnecessarily, and my temper does not become frayed and so that I do not hurt others. If I begin to get bored, I must think of ways and means to overcome boredom by doing something new and interesting. That way I will not bore others. I must then begin to organise my life better.

BLUE-PRINT FOR SUCCESS
Cultivate confidence and promote personality.

i. Realise here and now that you are a saleable commodity; that people are ready to buy you at your own cost.
ii. The time is now, for you to be true and sincere with yourself, to acknowledge all your faults, to recognise all the mistakes you have made in the past and those that you might still be making. Realign everything and move forward.
iii. The time is now, that all past experiences with negative people and personalities, and all past bad impressions and memories be buried, forgotten – and forgiven. Walk onwards with a clean slate. A mind etched with numerous scatters of agony depletes space, even that for stamping pleasant memories we ought to cherish. Allow henceforth; your mind to let go and gain power to only hold-on to what matters.
iv. Resolve here and now, as from today, that the past is past, that it is tomorrow for which you are planning. Ruminating on a series of hurtful past experiences, over and over again erodes your confidence, and might erase your dreams. Use your past as fuel to ignite an brighter future for yourself.
v. There is no reason on earth why you should not be a successful, confident and positive personality.
vi. Remove all padding on the problem; leave only bare things. The problem could be not as bad as it seems to be. Nothing cannot be solved if you put in the effort.
vii. Apply positive suggestive affirmations plus good thoughts to build up a mental picture of success.
viii. Turn this picture in the mind into actual material fact by taking positive, purposeful and immediate action. Never procrastinate.

CHAPTER VI

CHARACTER, SOCIAL LIFE AND ETHICS

Confidence, personality and success are all a result of the character of the individual. Character refers to the distinguishing features or quality of an individual (Pradhan, 2009). The way an individual conducts themselves is their character. Thus, character is the total sum of the way you look at life. This is how a man shows the way he thinks – by the way he looks, acts or behaves. Character also has a bearing on one's social life.

Social life is a humanity hobby. It is the result of scheming, planning, plotting, devising, inventing, creating and constructing. Social life also applies to any branch of activities that takes one away from home life and the work sphere. It encompasses the way of making friends, keeping them and doing extracurricular amusements with them. It's the creative sphere in which abilities and outlets not released at home or at work are given a chance to be expressed.

What is the third aspect for living? It is social life! Without the third aspect of living, work becomes monotonous. Solitude might as well turn up as too lonesome or somewhat boring. Thus, social activity is an escape, a release from frustrations and inhibitions. It supports togetherness and enables you to spread love in general, in as much as you receive it in turn. It fosters friendships and can spearhead creation of romantic bonds and marriages to some extent. Socialising develops speech and personality. A good and happy woman makes a good, happy wife. A good and happy man makes a good, happy husband. So, a good woman and a good man make a happy couple – thus any child will be an immediate reflection of them when born.

You ought to be a good mixer to have a healthy social life. Being a good mixer is a result of attitude, which is a result of one's confidence and self-esteem, and thus personality. It's not a chalkboard-teacher situation, but you get to learn quite a lot too, through interacting with others. If you value their companionship and maintain sincerity towards them, you'll reap the benefits. People you interact with can also make up your support network; and this helps a lot in times of need and unbearable stress, as discussed in other chapters. It helps to keep a sound stature of the mind.

Emotions, Morals, Conscience and Ethics in Personality Development

Many try hard to acquire wealth or create real, lasting success. That's absolutely pleasing, but to achieve these, emotions and feelings need to be guided by morality, conscience and ethics. Emotions and feelings, and their actions, have a direct impact on behaviour, and what's to be attained at the end. It is about making wise choices that you don't regret at a later stage. Avoid acting on impulse. Emotions point to what you feel, and they are variable. It is your moral sensitivity towards any particular situation, at any given time. Emotions do make life worth living. They have direct and indirect significant effects on our overall health as well. In other words, emotions are those feelings or mental reactions that an individual has in relation to any event. Feelings are the impressions of what you think.

Negative emotions can lead to poor bodily function… that is, the body also responds to the manner in which we think or feel in the mind – Chapter II covered this. According to research, this can cause or exacerbate some illnesses. So, when you feel you are alright and think you are in good condition, you'll find things working your way, and you'll become even more enthusiastic towards attempting ventures or just enjoying life in general. If you don't feel good emotionally, well, think again... think hard enough and long enough for there's always something to be appreciative about. The fact that you're alive and probably healthy means that you hold a great chance of making things right. There's always an opportunity to psyche your conscience and realign your moves. Set your ducks in a straight row and then move on. You are able, and you should always remember that.

A man is an animal in every respect, but his ability to judge right from wrong makes him rise above all ordinary animals, guided by conscience. Conscience is a little voice within a human being that tells us what is right and wrong. You need to be aware of that moment when you're about to cross that line of what's considered ethical – be it in business, friendships, relations, social life or any other personal endeavours.

Life Plan – One's Steps to Overhaul One's Conscience

Mental equipment is necessary for a successful overhaul of conscience.

Table 5: Overhaul of Conscience

Make a positive decision to overcome: ✪ Depression ✪ Defeatism ✪ Despondency ✪ Doubts *Have power to recognise these negative thoughts:* ✪ Egoism ✪ Embarrassment ✪ Evasiveness ✪ Eccentricity *Overhaul of conscience; a firm, immediate rejection of: –* ✪ Obsessive rituals ✪ Stubbornness ✪ Reclusiveness ✪ Self-righteousness/ Sanctimoniousness ✪ Self-adoration/narcissism	*Ability to recognise or appreciate contrasts:* ✪ Concentrate on a given job at a given time *Form positive judgement:* ✪ Put two plus two together and make a suitable whole. Your decisions must have weight/ meaning *Overcome negative thoughts:* ✪ Be able to identify right from wrong *Resolve to overcome:* ✪ Fear of failure ✪ Impulsive actions ✪ Guilt feeling from past errors ✪ Regression to childhood ✪ Excessive desires for protection/not being able to stand on your own ✪ Resolve to overcome inner conflicts with those with whom you deal

Now overhaul your conscience without reserve, to discover all personality faults from which you have suffered in the past and perhaps suffer from now, at this moment.

Overhaul of Conscience

How many people do I consciously hurt each day of my life? What little acts of dishonesty do I perpetuate from time to time? How many times am I cruel to the elderly, to children and animals? What lies do I tell to gain my own ends? Do I often take advantage of others when it suits me – exploit others, use them, or pick their brains? How much of my employer's time do I waste? How often do I lead others on with false promises or profess to know more than I do or to be able to do more than I can, especially when it involves the welfare of others? How mean, intolerant and small minded am I? How narrow-minded and improperly tight-laced am I? How class conscious do I get? How envious, jealous, covetous, extravagant am I? Am I a source of inspiration to anyone? Do I go way out to do anything that pleases my personality, completely disregarding others' feelings?

*As you answer these questions, try to figure out, if the same had been done to you, what kind of feelings would arise in you. Whatever you have done, was it morally justified? If not, there is need for a complete overhaul of your character and emotions.

Being Hurtful to Others

Surely, it is a failure of human nature to wound with words. We should know better. There's absolutely no need to provoke or emotionally hurt others. Calm, yet effective words are always there, available for us to use in expressing ourselves better when we are not satisfied with anything. The more hurtfully words are applied, the further the situation is likely to explode into something quite bad. However, even a single word can also be awful enough to cause damage. Imagine a cigarette butt thrown carelessly on a precious mountain, Table Mountain. It can, of course, destroy astounding amount of flora and fauna and can even spread farther to buildings. Not in your name. Be careful always. Once you train yourself not to be hurtful, it becomes an effortless, sound habit.

How many times, ask yourself, have you been guilty of intentionally hurting others? Sometimes, some people just get the desire to hurt and they wound deliberately. Strangely, it could be those people we love the most, or those individuals who truly love and look upon us whom we hurt the most. This is yet another bad behavioural pattern that can be found in humans and can never be condoned. It should not be allowed any room to grow. It all points inwards to vanity; the feeling that perpetrators experience in inflicting pain for perhaps pleasure, selfishness or undermining integrity of others, amongst other reasons.

Getting Yourself Appreciated

We all want to be appreciated by our mothers, fathers, brothers, sisters and the like. Now, to get appreciated you must appreciate others first; then they reciprocate your gesture and appreciate you in turn. There will be little they will not want to do for you. *Why?* This is because they will see themselves mirrored in you. Everybody likes looking in a mirror – and they smile especially when satisfied with the reflection they see. If you want others to appreciate you:

- You must stop insulting them.
- You must stop trying to boss them around.
- You must stop trying to correct them unnecessarily.
- You must try not to nag them.
- You must stop judging them.

Try a little cooperation. Do not show off. Do not try to make yourself more important than you really are. Again, do not preach. Do not force advice when it is unwanted or hasn't been requested.

Simply aim not to be *big-headed*. It erects a wall of enmity unnecessarily. When *big-headed,* you pretend to be superior, like you're knowledgeable about absolutely everything, and might deliberately try to make other people look or feel foolish. Big-headedness or uppishness could also be another person's only way out in trying to put themselves on top, because they'll fully know that they cannot climb up there directly – through their own earned stripes, hard work and acceptable strategic planning. No-one knows it all. No-one knows everything all the time. Relationships thrive better when all parties aspire to behave normally and be considerate towards one another. No bighead is a likeable personality anyway. A person with great attitude can be clearly distinguished; they have positive intentions, and they give well-informed suggestions.

If you're able to understand people, you can easily become popular. People love to be understood, listened to and have their input taken in for consideration. Understanding comes from experience in many cases, so do not shy away from acquiring experience, even when it hurts. Suffering a little, like everyone else going through the same phase, can also work greatly to your advantage. You'll then be able to relate and fully understand what others will be up to from time to time, should you happen to get a chance to climb up the ranks. Be open to reason; be a good listener and avoid only being nice to people when you want something from them – soliciting for favours!

One more important issue: make sure you mean something to someone. *Well, do you?* Being emotionally present for another person enhances their well-being and it boosts their happiness and gives them peace of mind. Togetherness is the most precious of states – you hardly ever see an ant moving around or working alone. Strings become stronger when interlaced into a pattern. To belong to someone, or to live for someone else too, is vitally important for your own personal happiness and growth as much as it'll be to the recipient. From the very moment we are born, we mean something to someone. Everybody is unique and special; thus, under normal circumstances... every individual is loved, and they too mean a lot to somebody.

FEEL CONTENTMENT

To feel fit, social-wise, is to be quite content with many things that we go through in life, especially those that involve others. If you were involved in an accident, for example, it's possible that you might perhaps feel there was much more you could have done to help and save other casualties. So, to compensate, you might begin to torture yourself by going back, over and over, reliving the event. The association of ideas gives rise to the symptoms of original shock; you will feel much as you felt shortly after the accident. Such practice should be ceased! It is harmful and quite unnecessary.

Flickers of guilt may also contribute towards slipping into depression. Depression can be generally described as sad feelings of gloom and inadequacy, according to a dictionary. It's important to be content with what you would have done, or rather promise yourself to do better next time, instead of living with regret. The moment has gone past now. We can only look to the future to get any previous mistakes rectified.

Party Preparations

Here are a few notes for a host or hostess to remember in case you decided to throw a party, in line with keeping your social life fun and active! Do not allow nervousness to discourage you one bit. Just keep it simple for a start. It could be a luncheon, a cocktail party, or a formal dinner with candles for only a few people – relatives or friends.

Party-giving demands. It pens one's personality, otherwise guests will not call again or give that party in return. Make every guest feel important and welcome. Make them feel how glad and grateful you are for their company and remember to introduce any individuals who are not well known within the gathering. It is important that they also acquaint themselves well with everyone else.

Do not be too ambitious, or experiment with dishes for the first time to impress guests with your culinary knowledge, unless you have capabilities or are fully exposed in the catering field. Get everything pre-planned, especially what you and your guests will do after the meal... games, watching a movie/series and the like. Know what drinks go with what dishes too, and when to serve them. All food dishes should be kept and served at their appropriate temperatures. You can't expose lettuce salad to direct sunrays, for instance; it quickly wilts and loses the oomph look. Keep canapés covered with plastic cling wrap to prevent them from drying out.

Voice!

Make it well-modulated, thus pleasantly pitched. Make it also loud enough to be heard above the party; but not raucous. Do not drop your voice at the end of the sentences.

Speech!
Always have something to say when you speak. Conversation is important, the priceless gift of the well liked. Do not talk about your children, the price of butter and bacon, your husband's job or anything that is irrelevant to the matter at hand. You might come across as unsettled or confused. Keep your mind calm and the flow of conversation will automatically fall into place, resulting in being effortlessly interesting.

Vocabulary!
Add to this but do not use words you think sound clever, but that are not commonly in use. Use only words that you fully understand. Do not confuse or embarrass your guests by using words that might be received with an awkward silence. Be simple in all that you say. Verbal communication is different from other forms of conveying messages. Avoid using slang whenever possible and do not crack risqué jokes. Teasing might be fun amongst friends or relatives, it can be great pastime, yes – spicing up relations, thus making moments even more enjoyable – but it can be malicious if taken too far and somebody could get hurt. Some jokes might turn out as sarcasm or a serious insult or may perhaps be deciphered as such. There's some hint of truth in jokes! One just needs to stay respectable at all times, not throwing out words without thought. By maintaining good relations, you also keep yourself away from unnecessary conflicts and burdens.

Sincerity!
Do not gush. It is artificial and no-one believes what you say. Be warm in the way you greet your guests and mean it. Some guests could be shy souls; make sure you have food passed to them more than once.

Ending the Party!
Ending a party may be a difficult task, especially when some of the guests still want to continue. Use language that indicates that it is okay to depart and remind them it won't be the last time you'll be throwing a party. There is a need to know when to be tactful and diplomatic. It may come across as rude too, frequently watching the clock or stipulating when certain guests need to get up in the morning, should they be sleeping over.

CHAPTER VII

CONFRONTING CHALLENGES HEAD-ON

Do not ever feel stuck in whatever mucky situation you might find yourself in or feel shackled by problems that may come along. Never allow your mind to be submerged under anxiety; look out for that silver lining orbing around the difficulty – there's always one. Identify it and shake yourself as quickly as you can and bounce back onto track. To reach greater heights, we sometimes need to walk on rough roads, even some with traps of thorns randomly set along the route. Solve problems to the best advantage and in a way that enables you to propel forward. There's growth and maturity to be gained out of solving problems successfully.

Everybody has their own sounds. You make them with the things you do every day. They are the sounds that formulate your personal signature. These are the sounds with which those nearest and closest to you identify you. With that said, do not let anxiety make you an addict! Addiction to drinking alcohol, smoking, indulging in unsafe sex and consuming wrong foods. If you have become a drink addict, or a chain smoker, or a habitual over eater, or you are unable to control your sex urges, trying to remove – or even succeeding in removing – these habits and addictions might not be a lasting solution. You will have to track down the cause, which is, of course, the underlying anxiety responsible for your attempted escape from reality. It could take a very long time and immense effort to get back on track. Please avoid starting in the first place. Do not shy away from facing problems and challenges head-on.

Drink might make you lose your fears by inhibiting anxieties, but problems still remain unsolved. It'll be merely temporary numbing of the mind. Smoking to excess may steady your nerves, *so you think,* but problems go unsolved. So, you get to drink more and more and you smoke more and more. You wear yourself out with these things and in the end, *where are you?* You still have problems. Do not let your anxiety make you an addict.

No matter that you may mislead yourself in thinking that your anxieties do not exist, you always know at the rock bottom of your heart that they do. These anxieties begin to press on you more and more. So, you will have to drink more heavily, smoke much more, resort to physical pleasures more frequently in a vain attempt to win the race – always trying to keep yourself that little bit ahead of your worries. You could have been running away from problems, yes, in your thinking, but that won't be the reality of things. It'll be simply superficial. Addictions will only leave you in very poor shape, mentally and physically. You could even risk losing all the ability or faculties of resistance to be able to help yourself overcome the situation... a double trouble scenario! You then become hopelessly lost, should you fail to get help from outside.

The longer you run away from solving problems, the less likely you will ever be able to solve them. Fighting against perplexities and problems of life keeps you in good practice. If you get on well, the time comes when you will have next to no problems. Just stay alert and be ready to nip them in the bud – immediately that they begin to show up.

When your senses are dulled by alcohol and tobacco, nicotine or by insidious urge for sexual excitement, it seems you have no problems. How can you possibly hope to be clear minded enough to cope with problems, settle your anxieties and be worry free, if you are not able to solve your own problems in a timely manner? You will end up having an evasive personality. People will begin to lose confidence in you. They cannot rely on you in a crisis. They will not come to you for last-minute decisions. You cannot be a leader or trusted to handle any decision-making positions.

Evaluate Your Habits and Associations

Habits are behavioural patterns that are frequently repeated – successfully in stable conditions (Klockner & Prugsamatz, 2012). Mixing in bad company can become an association – a habit. Such inclinations are personality destroying. They are at the outset of anti-social behaviour. Any habit or custom that goes against the normal requirements agreed upon within society is negative, and its effects are against the creation of a confident or positive outlook.

Bad habits can be difficult to change because they are due to cognitive processes; it is all in the mind (Jager, 2003). Therefore, there is a need to change one's mindset to be able to break the mould. When bad habits need to be broken there has to be a strong desire to do so. A chain smoker, for instance, may not want to stop his vice; neither may a drinker or a woman chaser, when not entirely ready to do so. The habit could be very deeply rooted, to the extent that the victim would have lost all desire for self-reformation.

Nevertheless, once a person seeks to break away from a bad habit, the battle is half won already! First, he must rid himself of the mentality of not wanting to break the habit; he then must begin breaking away from habit itself. There are two battles to be fought. Mental attitude must be changed, then the object of obsession must be gradually removed until the desire no longer exists. After the ability to break habits has been achieved, commanding attention in any situation will be possible. Always have the desire and drive to better yourself at every sunrise.

Learn to Solve Problems Instantly

If you are the sort of person whose subconscious mind communicates well with the conscious mind easily, or you're able to apply reflective thinking effectively, then you may have an aptitude for solving problems more easily than most. You get enough opportunity to formulate the best possible decision. If you are a thinker, taking pains over detail, you probably tackle problems very carefully, thereby leaving no stone unturned in finding a sound solution.

If you develop a habit of shying away from solving problems in a timely way, you'll find yourself cowering or getting excessively anxious as soon as you sense or see any of them looming in sight. Look upon a problem as a challenge to your intellect and intelligence and reasoning powers. Well, life would be a pretty dull place if there were no problems here and there. The mind would become dulled and perception would never be used. Problems are puzzles. They're indeed a pen and pencil job – they are to be worked out.

Staying Focused and Having Dreams

Imagine you are looking down a long tunnel... at the end of which is a bright light. You can see nothing else but that bright light at the end of the tunnel. A man can see one thing at a time when focused, and visibility becomes very prominent.

Well, with that said, what you dream about in your sleep is the negative of your black and white photographed conscious life. Dreams usually draw attention to what we need and desire as individuals. They are therefore unique. Introspection should be good enough in evaluating a possible meaning of all of them in relation to your life. Dreams are supposed to bring about healing and perhaps help us to resolve our inner struggles. They should not torment the mind.

Some fall into debt in the quest to find the meanings of dreams. It is not necessary to waste time and money in trying to find interpretations of mere dreams unless in the case of nightmares that may require talking to a loved one or consulting with a counsellor. The moment you allow your mind to worry and mull over dreams, over and over again, this accords them room to make you feel blue by raising anxiety levels unnecessarily. That cripples your power of having to focus on important issues. Be, therefore, blinkered like a horse on a track, which is not distracted by trivialities in its quest for success.

> *"Watch your thoughts; they become words. Watch your words; they become actions. Watch your actions; they become habits. Watch your habits; they become your character. Watch your character; it becomes your destiny."* – FRANK OUTLAW

CHAPTER VIII

LIFE OF A CONFIDENT ADULT INDIVIDUAL

I AM WOMAN

Your name is so small,
It looks incomplete
Just 'M a n'
Mine;
Larger and rhythmic it is –
A welcome serene tonal pattern...
Seeping through a commotion,
I am 'W o m a n'
Prefixing yours
My name, respectfully starting with 'Wo',
It's the Womb that nurtures and makes the
World flourish
Womanhood it is!
It's complete
The name 'Woman' ornaments the status,
Culinary art of spicing
Although to this world I came later than you
Pityingly, God had found you incomplete
The predominant holy book on land stresses and sympathises...
I am Woman and there
To complete!
Our unity,
Symmetrical and steadfast – like
Ceaseless complete dietary course,

Glistens and sparks additional cubits to life span
Generation, swinging to another
Nothing could be solider and sublime…

I am Woman;
A Mother
And Aunt
To sons and daughters
Yet a daughter and niece
The sister to him and her
"Cousin!" others call me
I enlace affection in the family, so to share with the world at large
I'm still that being who bears pain of crying souls –
A pricking pillow to dream on
I fully understand the pain and triumph
Of introducing an innocent soul to the world
I am a watchful Neighbour!

Certified by nature to enrich the World, I'm 'Her'
And to better the World is 'He' and 'She'
Concomitantly
It's 'You' and 'I'
Without me – despair
Dizziness of wandering on unknown lands
And I, without You,
I hold no purpose
And the World is
Naught…

– AUXIE MZIL-LEHANG

A confident family man has a happy home. He is confident that he is keeping his family to the best of his ability; confident in his love and affection for every member of his household; and confident of the future for himself and all of them. This is born of inner calm, a sense of responsibility, a mature outlook that married life should bring. It is not necessarily a product of a four-figure income, not at all! Happiness in married life does not have to be based on personal power, possession, or prestige. A lot of people might think happiness means cash, power and prestige. Alright, let's be realistic: *who doesn't want any of these things, anyway?* The simple take for me may be no worries, no responsibilities. Let's say money is good, but great power is the last word happiness could call for.

All the same, be wary of the person who prefers the simple things in life. He is taking the line of least resistance. Hard work and perseverance bring out the best out of an individual, create creative thinking and make goals well worth reaching. If you want true happiness, go and get it, work for it, do not run away from the complexities of existence – puzzles amuse and solutions satisfy. Happiness is the way you look at your life: accept it and self-adjust to look at it your way.

Your Children!

A crosscheck exam for positive inspirational growth in being a responsible and confident parent:

- Are you as a parent too strict?
- Are you over-spoiling your offspring?
- Does it feel like they'll be young forever?
- Do you train/expose them to responsibilities according to their growth stages?

- Are they aware that one day they'll have to fend for themselves?
- Are you preparing them along that route?
- Do you give them too much freedom?
- Do you cover up for whatever wrongs they have done, moving on like nothing ever happened?

You cannot be anxiety driven when dealing with children. Lack of confidence in yourself as the disciplinarian might lead to a child ending up taking the reins and ruling over you – doing as they please. The latter might have serious consequences in the development of the child, including how they view and treat other adults outside the family sphere, like at school, for example. Their minds are still maturing; an adult should know better, hence should operate constructively. You've been a youngster before, but children do not possess the experience of being an adult. When your children have no confidence in you as the parent or guardian, *won't that lead to domestic crisis?* How are you training them to face life without you standing next to them? What are you doing to help them face the future, confident and ready?

There's absolutely nothing wrong with sharing your past experiences with children, depending on their level of understanding, but it's not necessary to enforce rules on them on the basis of what happened to you in your past era. These teens have nothing to do with your past; they do not care, because these are their own current days they are in; things will be different in many ways. Lifestyles will have shifted, and they could be earning even more than you did in your teen days. They have more ventures to explore than yesteryear. They usually develop more quickly – mentally, and physically to some extent. They dress differently too. Their lives are influenced by trends in many cases, movies, cartoons, novels, fashion and so on. A little fun is always good, so long as it's not harmful. What they require is positive guidance, so that they do not get carried away or lose direction or operate under peer pressure. The penultimate goal is to cheer and support them so that they, too, realise and accomplish their own dreams. That way, it fuels them up – and they will contribute even more to humanity.

ARE YOU CONVINCED?

Do you know what you want out of life? How far back was it when you first started getting ambitions? At school, at your first job or do you want anything out of life at all apart from reasonable security, comfort, spending money, and a roof over your head? That's not really ambition. Those are the things anyone can reasonably expect out of life.

Some women are ambitious for a man with money, a home with good things in it and children, a contented home life and later on grandchildren. On the other hand, *some men are ambitious for* a woman who can be a mother, sister and wife – all in one – a neat conventional home plus just enough money to keep it going, friends to hang out with, then children and later on grandchildren. Perhaps a retirement pension will also make it onto the list.

There's absolutely nothing wrong with the discussed, but having normal ambitions means you are more likely to lead a contented life. Contentment can, however, result in tormentingly boring scenarios sometimes. It lacks excitement, effort and achievement. Besides, you never make your mark if you are too contented. You live and die, having contributed nothing much to humanity. Go on and challenge yourself to reach very high!

Accomplish as much as you can and avoid setting limits. Once one level is reached, don't settle – leap to the next one!

Why not even create for your progeny? They can stand and grow from what you have created. Whatever you want out of life – a shop of your own, a business of your own, a name as a creative writer, artist, composer, designer, programmer, industrialist – whatever it is; it all lies in your talent and passion, and it is all upon you as an individual to attain it. You must first of all be able to visualise it and see it as an accomplished mission. Seeing is believing in what you want to achieve. Practically everything that can be visualised can be realised. The magnetism of desire is a very powerful force; its function is to attract and to draw towards one that which is most desired! If you visualise anything, make sure you really want it and have true passion for it. If your heart wants it, make sure you can get it; if you manage to get it, make sure you keep and grow it further.

How Early in Life Should You Start Trying to Accomplish Your Particular Ambition?

When you have shaken the dust of the classroom off; when you have really begun to live after you have suffered a little; when you have some adult responsibilities; when others have begun to look up to you for support; when you know you are a responsible individual; and when you can sort out day-dreams from reality, fishing fantasy from fiction. In short... when you truly feel you've reached the stage of maturity.

According to many scientific sources like that of Professor Louann Brizendine, a neuropsychiatrist who wrote *The Female Brain*, females mature earlier than their counterparts, cognitively and physically to some extent. Mostly, their emotional make-up adjusts itself more quickly. In as much as men take a bit longer to mature, it cannot be used as an excuse or as a shield to run away from responsibilities. For many individuals, a line is drawn because some men are susceptible to getting overly dependent for too long on a mother, sister and wife image to help guide them, feed and refresh them, and clean up after them – amongst other things. I have seen it too in my three decades of work experience in the field of homeopathy as well as when serving my local community.

"My wife doesn't cook on time", "My wife cannot iron properly", "My wife ___." I've heard this kind of thing many times, from carpers, and I always ask back... aren't the two supposed to be complementing each other? If one party reaches to a certain level, should the other not complete it? Filling in any void, so that they rise to that particular level which satisfies both of them! Working together harmoniously begins with modest gestures towards one another in our small spaces.

A man can feel he is mature when he can stand on his own feet and do without the ministrations of his mother. Cynics will say he will immediately search out another suitable 'mother' upon moving out of his parents' home. So lost is he without a female person forever in the background that he will seek out another woman, expecting her to execute almost the same, or even the exact, duties his mother used to do for him when he was younger. Well, that is in the final discussion, the main drive behind some men, and his ambition to get a partner who, although he may wish to deny it, will be a mother image rather than his better half.

There used to be a belief in the past that every woman becomes a mother as soon as she marries, and her first child will be the husband. In that matter, cynics will likely sit back and relax, allowing their cynicism to flourish further. Every man must have absolute respect for women. A woman is the greatest inspiration life has to offer. A woman has the capacity to give a man the chance to project his ego by bearing his child or children – the extension of his physical self.

When you marry, that automatically becomes a union. Marriage is about sharing, building one another and companionship. It is structured upon a foundation of love. When marriage is viewed in such rightful manner, matrimonial days should always be beautiful. Being cynical or abusive towards your partner will equally taint your 'meant to be' rosy days, as much it will affect your better half and your children.

Some of the biggest successes in life have had women behind them. It is about helping each other achieve or become the best human beings you each can be. Have you now got an idea of whether you must marry to be successful or be successful enough to marry? Do not get confused; you can be ambitious and succeed all alone, if you wish to. Be sure of what you want out of life; see it in your mind's eye and be certain you'll be able to stick to the commitment. Perhaps you're already working towards achieving your objectives; going all out there to fetch the necessary tools you require. Well, keep at it! Never expect anything great to happen too quickly, though. You might be left utterly disappointed and discouraged.

In your twenties, life is first beginning to take on meaning. You have discovered who you are: an intellectual, an individualist, a go with the masses or a go ahead... amongst other qualities. *In your thirties,* you have assumed responsibilities and people have come to depend on you. *In your forties,* you have begun the most fruitful, productive part of life. Half a lifetime of experience is behind you. You have perhaps suffered, and know what it is to suffer, to want, to strive, to struggle and to work hard. You have overcome probably many disappointments, and are now fully aware of how nerve-wracking it can be to regret. You have probably lost loved ones too. You could have had no peculiar opportunities that you can possibly observe. You may as yet not felt influential people or any close ones cheering you on. *You know what?* Success can come at any age, what you require is persistence. Never give up on yourself and do not let circumstances smother your dreams. Do not allow time to erode your passion and what you envision for yourself. Ultimate power to drive your aspirations to fruition lies entirely in your hands. Keep it alive and work on it.

By this time, in your forties, if you are going to be a success you should be well on your way. Look ahead. Set the forties as a reasonable time at which you should be well on the way to success. Prizes are greater today than they used to be a while back. There is more money to be earned and more opportunities to take advantage of. Many industries have been created in the fashion, materials, agriculture, science, tourism, and entertainment fields... to name a few.

The greatest item at the onset is to be convinced of what you want, and to distinguish what you are cut out to be. Know and acknowledge what you can do better than anything else and maximise on it. That is it.

How Are You To Know What You Want Is Right?

- If it helps you forward, you are right.
- If it makes your life happier without bruising other people's rights, you are right.
- If it keeps you fit and well, you are right.

- If it is honest and above board, you are right.
- If it helps others forward too, you are right.
- If its spiritual aims are good, you are right.
- If its moral aspects are above reproach, you are right.
- If it is tangibly good, you are right.
- If it is mentally invigorating, you are right.

Cultivating Happiness and the Art of Happy Living

- Try to always reason calmly.
- Analyse constructively.
- Calculate the chances of cultivating sure success out of every situation.
- Weigh up the odds against you and compare with things in your favour and draw an honest conclusion.
- Assess the effects, should your plans not come to fruition.
- Evaluate the implications of ultimate success.
- Enlist favourable cooperation should a need possibly arise.

The art of happy living is to confidently expect the best. Go on, work towards it and achieve. What you desire can be drawn to you if you keep your focus on target. Remain true to yourself and observe all the moral principles; it'll work out. What can be imagined out of thin air can be turned to reality. Hopes can be realised and wishes bounce into life. People you want to be affiliated with, money/wealth you need to earn or make can be earned if worked for passionately and strategically. Possessions you covet can be made to become yours. Power can be won. Prestige can be gained. Personality can be promoted by suggesting to yourself that it will be so; assuring yourself that it will be so and seeing it as so.

What an unmoving and silent place the world would be if it were not for this great evocation power to plan and execute. As real as sound and light waves are, so are thought waves! They can be transmitted in similar manner and received in just the same way as that of sound and light. They can be turned into power in just the same way, otherwise what would be the meaning of life at all? We would probably be vegetables or simply living and operating only on instinct. There would be no clear direction, no conditions, no fulfilment, no fun or urge to climb toward any accomplishments, no sense of competition and no effort if we do not set ourselves to doing something... and specifying when.

How many people grasp this great power with open arms? How many truly care? Some might be content with their situations and not aspire to anything huge. That's okay, but setting challenging goals for oneself keeps the mind agile and active. Simply having them set enriches life and provides defined direction to follow, and fulfilling the dreams brings elaborated joy to the heart as well as a sensational feeling of satisfaction. You keep developing and amassing wealth of knowledge and experience too, changing the world for better, even if it's just within the immediate space around you. Individuality can become a lost cause if you just sit back and watch other people shape the world in their own spheres of interest. The spirit of adventure dies a quick death.

CHAPTER IX

HOW NOT TO BE INFLUENCED BY WHAT OTHERS SAY OR DO

They may try to mislead you out there, as to your true capabilities. Fight this! They may try to veer you into false emotionalism... see through all this. They may try to attack your weakest and most vulnerable mental and physical spots. This, you must guard against. They may try to twist your words just to break your character – remain firm and stay true to who you really are. They may try to mould your personality to their own liking. Resist this! *What an utter waste of meant-to-be good life if you let such things affect you.*

Your personality is your own property and can be developed only by you. You live for no-one else but *you*. They may try to make you feel sad or bad: by implication, by deed, by ignoring you, or by delegating energy/authority elsewhere. When you rightfully belong to yourself, and with full understanding of your own purpose, then who are they that you must effortlessly try to conform to them?

Are you prepared, deviating from your own goals and ambitions to satisfy malefic remarks or attitudes? Those with whom you associate depend upon you for progress: your family, your close friends, the people with whom you work. New people you meet could be those who may want to pull you down; whose thoughts, deeds and actions may negatively influence you and might rob you of your personality and confidence. Social media hasn't made it any easier either. It came along with its own perils trailing behind the good.

Please do not be dismayed, meeting up or interacting with new people; it can be amazing indeed, and that's how relations are usually formed. It is a wonderful experience – extending your horizons and expanding your territories. Just keep your positivity well-insulated, bullet-proofed from any missiles of negativity. The world is full of different characters: some disappointed, frustrated, inhibited, compulsion-ridden folks, inclined towards destroying others with whom they come into contact. This is because they cannot accept seeing successful or progressing individuals. That is the negative influence of hetero-suggestion, wickedly at work now and then. Of course, there are good influences too, sometimes, depending on the situation.

Hetero-suggestion can also be inspiring, making us improve ourselves for the better and thereby prospering in life. There are friends and members of your family who wish no harm, who help you wholeheartedly, who would not criticise or mentally maim you. Even those good folks are guilty at times, occasionally exerting a negative influence over you. Perhaps not intentionally, but through careless and thoughtless stances. They probably do not understand the power of negative suggestions. They tell you that you look dull, ill, pale, under the weather, too fat or too thin, as soon as they glance at you, after not having seen you in a while, for example. They say you do not look as young as you used to. You must rest up a bit more; you cannot expect to be able to do as much as you used to do. They pose random questions; ask if you have a headache, or if your stomach aches.

You might then begin to develop negative feelings about yourself. You'll probably start torturing yourself in the mind, instead of focusing on the plus side. Learn to dwell on the rosy side of aspects and cull all negativity that holds no value. You take a series of pictures with your smartphone and you realise afterward that you're not quite impressed with some of them… *wouldn't you just select them and press delete?* As easy as that: discard all negativity thrown in your path.

Ordinary day-to-day encounters too, do carry negative connotations sometimes and can easily dampen one's spirits when not placed under guard. You read such on social media platforms. You see it transpiring on the buses, in trains, in the streets; quite often, you hear stories of failure – I did not make it, I failed, I lost, he turned me down, oh, what a puzzling world… They said I was not good enough, too young, too old, too little experience and so on. There is not enough money coming in. I do not know how we shall manage. Pete, my uncle's friend's cousin, is down with a cough. All these are negative. Do not worry. We can be compassionate, yes, but do not allow it to affect you. If you are a positive personality type, you can and will overcome internalising all such negative talk.

How? You may ask.

This is by remembering that it all starts in the mind: the other person's mind. How on earth, why on earth does what goes on in another person's mind affect you if you do not want it to? Quite ridiculous! If you were listening to the radio and did not want to receive a certain station, would you not switch off the radio or tune into a different station? If you do not want to receive a certain thought, or hear a particular line of talk, you just do not give it the platform to affect your mind. *That is all.* You will turn a deaf ear, rather. You can run away from the harshness of life that makes you feel powerless by shutting out a thought, or a scene, or an occurrence, or a happening that you hate or find disturbing.

Your mind can become a complete blank. Refuse whatever discrete item, and the mind will entirely reject it for you. Commiserate and help strengthen your loved ones, who receive these negative thoughts by allowing their beautiful minds to be manipulated in negative ways. Some individuals are merely mental sadists, obtaining pleasure from inflicting mental torture on others. Let them play their little twisted games. When someone tries to attack your integrity, assure yourself you are more sensible, well balanced, plus emotionally mature... which you are! You understand your purpose and you know what you want, and the means to get it!

So, you learn how to switch on to only positive suggestions and not to open up to negative interferences. There's so much positivity in the world that allowing room to pile up negativity becomes a waste and hindrance to living a sound life. This is where you start with the positive tonic talk – talk discussed in the coming sections and use as counter-blows to atonic talk. There's a difference in tone and speech of someone who is sincerely concerned to that of an individual who has intentions of just pulling others down.

So, if you were told that you look ill, but you know you're not, say, "I look and feel fit". If you were told you will fail, speak success. Say, "I will not fail."

Tell this to yourself and to the other person as well. Probably, he is used to everyone wilting under his negative suggestions, succumbing to his potent atonic talk, that he is conditioned to having his own way all the time. You can deflect the stance. Talk right at him and he will be surprised. He will begin to see how well you really look. He will see that healthy colour in your cheeks. He will see how impossible it is for you to fail. He will give in, alright... You will be well. You will look good and you will succeed. He will begin to tell you this, and so he tells himself. Two can always play this game of wits. There's absolutely no need for you to ever clench a fist: you're too smart for that. Double lock this in your cognition chest.

Again, do not be negatively influenced by all you read in the papers, see on television, or read on the internet – the new blood of today's digitally-driven lifestyles! Some people in the act of posting stuff could be generally scared of losing their money invested in whatever their line of business lies, or scared of jeopardising their jobs, prestige, popularity and so forth. Have a strong stance and learn to sift the good from the bad. Not everything is bad; not everything is good. Allow your rational judgement to lead you; only fish out what's of importance to you as an individual. Do not operate under the drive of peer pressure because our lives are all different and unique.

What would you risk losing, operating under the drive of peer pressure?

You might end up falling into debt in the case of chasing after endless things, in trying to keep up with every bit and piece that steals your heart; getting carried away with every click of the mouse or flip of a page. Debt can also trigger mental distress and depression, and that may lead to a negative change in your overall behaviour. Keep away. With that said, try to avoid purchasing items on a credit basis, as much as you can. If whatever item you're about to purchase depreciates in value; contemplate. Ask yourself twice if it's a wise idea in that instance to opt for credit. It may be better to accumulate money, bit by bit, until you're able to pay cash for the item! That way you'll also be able to fully understand and appreciate what's really of value to you. You are unique in your own right, wouldn't it make sense that you design your own precedences, and then stick to them?

You'd also risk losing dignity, pride in yourself, power and principles too, at the expense of listening and applying negative forces of the outside to your own life through peer pressure or incautious moves. You could lose a lot too – faith, health and wealth. Some hetero-suggestion ideas are consciously calculated to wreck your hopes, sabotage success, or pull you down in your prime. Be aware and well informed always. You ought to be diligent in each and every move you make. All that glitters is not necessarily gold, as an old saying goes.

In general, many of us are scared of fire outbreaks, wars and pandemics. These bring about fatalities and a lot of instability in some situations, as well as uncertainty. Some of these personal, social, industrial, spiritual, political and military catastrophes are brought about by negative hetero-suggestion. The human element is always behind it all in many cases. The minus influence/negative suggestions play a great part in the lives of literally everyone, unless perhaps when one lives like a nut in the pod – entirely shut away from the realities of the outside world. It is difficult, yes, running away from all the effects of hetero-suggestion, but some people are always ready to expect the worst, and of course they somehow attract it to themselves by so doing... all because there's power in what you tell yourself. Always expecting the worst might also lead you into making ridiculously small mistakes that may end up being costly to fix.

The minus influence starts working as soon as one wakes in the morning. Very few people, except babies and teenagers in love, wake up each day feeling completely full of the joys of life. There is a strong tendency to review the mistakes and failures of yesterday, even before the electric shaver has been plugged in, hair dryer switched on, or the morning coffee water is on the boil.

Yesterday is the first thing we think of; what happened, what was worrying us as we fell asleep last night. How much money did we lose yesterday? How much work did we manage to get through? How much is left to tackle today? What will so and so be thinking after what we said to him yesterday? How much are we even going to manage to accomplish today, from the lot we failed to do yesterday?

After a while, when more oxygen has travelled to our brain, we begin to sort out the subconscious worries and the negative thoughts – allowing our sensible conscious mind to take over. That is the dawn of reason. From that moment onwards we must begin to sort the grain from the chaff. Reject the negative thoughts and accept the positive promise for the new day. It is those who are unable to let the sane, conscious mind take over who quickly fall victim to negative hetero-suggestion that focuses them to accept failure at the outset, even before it has had time to set in. When you first wake up in the morning, set the theme for the day going in a positive manner by dismissing what happened yesterday that was not first and foremost good. Set yourself up for a brighter and happier day!

WHEN NEGATIVE HETERO-SUGGESTION THREATENS

Every human being is an entity to himself and commands himself. He is himself and no-one can rob him of that. His thoughts, actions, words and works stem from him and him alone. However, he can fall prey to outside influences. It is up to each of us whether we open up to negativity or remain firm – staying wholly positive, all the time, every day, all our life. No mind should be so soft or pliable – like dough, or ductile like copper, which can be easily modelled to produce pretty bracelets to robust industrial machinery. Outside influences can completely rob it of its individuality, stripping it of its personality or smothering its positive powers of progression. Hold fast to your integrity with honour.

When negative hetero-suggestion threatens, remember *not to accept it*. Protect yourself with calmness from within. Walk away, talk, or do something to change the mood and tempo. Summon reserves of will power. Turn a deaf ear, refuse, and reject! Relax as soon as possible – mentally and physically. Allow the calm and soothing waters of rational reasoning to engulf you, and allow the serene power of resilience to serenade you with notes of strength and wellbeing.

You can do this: yes, you're able. Your mind has strength that is stronger then the currents of antagonism. Deny the presence of adverse or contemptuous criticism. Do not allow it room to sit for much longer on your mind; it could have been spearheaded by a defect in one's character. Stay out of circulation until you are sure of any self-doubts. Wait until all unpleasantness has passed and know that you are still as positive as you were before the attack.

You may likely fall victim to what others say because their message and your thoughts are in conflict. Then, you may easily give in to their negative suggestions, although at the back of your mind you know that the words are antagonistic to what you really like or had planned for yourself. You might also lose the battle because you have cultivated an incorrect attitude towards yourself and now you're only focusing on what other people think of you – neglecting your own principles. Anything you may want to do, you start looking for validation from others first, which won't always be a great move; you're simply approaching them out of fear of what they may say about you! If you suffer from a feeling of doubt about your inner strengths and abilities or accomplishments, the battle not to block negative hetero-suggestion might be hard, but can be achieved if you work on it.

OVERCOMING NEGATIVITY

There's a need to formulate correct and strong values for your own personal life and condition the mind to brace up against negative criticisms and victimisation; and not be easily hurt by what the next person says or thinks of you. Do not get into a self-pity syndrome. *Why would you?* That may rob you of your confidence, creating a void that could make you become prey and more susceptible to succumb to any negativity passed. It can cause damage to other innocent relations, your general health and well-being, as well as affecting your work. Tell yourself the following:

- I have a strong desire to overcome all negative opposition.
- I will cultivate only positivity to make myself blossom.
- I will make the most of all today has to offer.
- I will enjoy every moment of today and tomorrow, and the next day!
- I will be content with this day.
- I will not yearn for what's not reachable, or what I cannot obtain immediately.
- I will make the most of what I have.
- I will add more love to my life and be gentler with myself.
- I will understand people better.
- I will try to understand myself even better.

⊙ I will try to meditate more and increase my mental awareness.

BOREDOM

Boredom is an evil minus influence that, at its extremes, convinces us there is nothing to live for, nothing to do, nowhere to go, no new friends to be found, nothing creative or worthwhile to do, nothing new to learn, and the like. Boredom is born of several factors and amongst them are health issues, discontentment and falling short of fresh ideas. Thus, monotony and boredom attack people variedly. It may come to people who are in the house all day, to an individual in a dead-end job, or to an idler. Realistically, no-one needs to be bored if there is something to do that possesses a creative element. You can do some good for someone, even if it is only by yourself. Do some home gardening, another example. There's nothing as heart-warming as witnessing plants grow, and seeing them flourish with bright flowers – then sniff their sweet scent!

The power of auto-suggestion also comes into play in keeping oneself bouncy. This is what you tell or assure yourself. Speak positively to yourself and nourish your mind with aspirations. It can become a habit – an interesting one – sooner than you'd realise.

Hetero-suggestion, like auto-suggestion, is responsible in many ways for the creation of happiness or boredom. People might say or pose supposedly weird questions to you, for instance, "Are you not bored being at work all day long?" "Doesn't that monotonous job bore you?" They suggest to you and you may end up developing some negativity if you do not hold strongly enough to your ideals. The list goes on and on... "Doesn't having nothing much to do bore you?" "Aren't you bored having so much money to spend, or so little to spend?" "That job you just landed will definitely bore you very soon!" "Doesn't the show bore you? I see you watching it over and over?" "I see you wear green all the time. Don't you get bored?"

Tell you what... pretty soon you'll likely be bored stiff, all because people have told you that you will be bored, and you have allowed your mind to believe them. Strength of mind is crucial, as is being able to withhold all that you planned for yourself and see yourself ticking off boxes of what you set for yourself.

Simple changes to try and overcome menace influences of boredom that make routine feel monotonous, and the daily grind repetitive, include stimulating your mental resourcefulness by incorporating something that is constructively active, either mentally or physically. When you are working, allow your mind to piece together what you are going to do later on, after work. Feel that what you are doing at that moment is worthwhile too, and you'll still be achieving something real and concrete at the end of the task. Allow everything you do to add a little to your knowledge. Each moment of every day could and should be full of existence that has never happened before. Cash in on those moments. Make the most of them. You'll have done yourself good without a doubt.

Try out new hobbies too. Nothing brings out personality as well as the development of a new hobby or interest outside normal daily routine. It gives one something new to look forward to each day. It matters not how small it might be; it suffices. People with things to do that please them are seldom bored. If somebody hits you with negative suggestions, feel sorry for their lack of perception; you know yourself much better and exactly what you are up to!

Do not allow people to stream to you all the negatives said about you by other people. It weighs down unnecessarily sometimes, and that'll be a waste of precious time. It can bring about boredom too, and boredom robs you of your personality. You will become flat, sluggish and might lose sparkle. *How then will you be able to accomplish your dreams in such a state?* Have the power to reject this before your voice falls tuneless. You surely wouldn't want your eyes growing dull; too dull to appreciate the beauty of life and all the opportunities the world has to offer. You can never give in to walking with a stoop in the name of isolated individuals who are not walking the same journey as yours. Smile, laugh hard and step out with a spring in your step! You are adequate – and belong to this world, just like everyone else.

You, however, have a responsibility too, not to be a bore to others. You wouldn't bear that countered against you either. Do not monopolise conversation and avoid talking down others. Do not assume you have a green light flashing for you always. Do not brag about what you have done or what you intend to do. Do not be an antagonist and try to start purposeless rows. Do not smear or scandalise anyone – or about anything that belongs to someone else. Do not assume every advice that you might be considering as great will come out equally important to others. Be careful of everything you say so that it won't rob you of your personality. Good manners are the very essence of a pleasing personality.

CHAPTER X

YOU'RE THE SALESMAN OF YOUR OWN LIFE

Car dealerships sell vehicles, a musician sells music, the minister sells the Good Word of God, the doctor sells good health and the psychologist, amongst other professions, sells good thoughts. *You* – zooming out your individuality – can sell your own good self to the world! Know what you can do better than all else.

Identify your particular line of specialty. Find out where what you can do best fits in. Evaluate if you can possibly benefit from it; turning your skill and passion to profit. Work on that which you feel you do best; sharpen the craft, so as to be able to be competitive in the identified work sphere. Get to know people active in that particular area or field. See yourself as one of them. Sell yourself to them – that you're capable and can complement what they're doing. Or get advice on how you can possibly go about reaching your particular target market. Sell yourself to them. Yes! Life is salesmanship.

Everyone who is engaged in the business of living is literally selling himself or herself to the next influential person willing to buy him or her. It'll be a projection of 'artistry in oneself', and that's basically the product you'll be selling in every case. Positive thoughts and the power of projection are the salesman's chief weapons, as indeed they are ours too, in selling ourselves to the world. Negative thoughts, however, may chip in. They are conveyed by the flush of hesitant manner, procrastination and daunted feelings. In the beginning of every sales interview, the air might be tight and heavy with negative thoughts, but everything eases up as time ticks away – and the flow gets easier and smoother as the parties involved gain confidence in each other. It has happened to others through the success of their businesses, or their lives in general. There is no reason on earth why it should not happen to you – whatever profession you are in – at any given age.

What Would Make You Fail to Sell Yourself Successfully?

Is your problem perhaps mentioned down here?

Emotionally mixed up, less than principled, closed-minded, always fumbling for a legitimate means of escaping responsibilities, insecure, unsure, undeveloped emotionally, mother fixated type/overly reliant on other people, undeveloped mentally, escapist from reality, willing to take – but reluctant to share, scared to execute own ambitions, fear of failure, fault finding, jealousy, unsure, feel inferior, easily led/crowd follower, frustrated, self-centred, anti-social, a hypochondriac to the extent of feeling scared to move out of the comfort zone, an escapist, generally negative, an obstructionist, having a persecution complex, pessimist, self-pitying character, unsteady, delusional, always confused, emotionally insecure, anxious, complex determinist, lacking spiritual security, irresponsible, mean-spirited, ambitious but too negative to take further steps.
All the above need to be turned over to an idealistic, high principled and emotionally strong stature to make it in selling yourself to the world.

CAN YOU BE A SUCCESS IN LIFE?
Can you design a fabulous mansion? Can you speak more than one language? Can you act certain characters? Sing pop or gospel music... perhaps?

Changing career midstream when married is pretty risky, unless incorporated and fitting into what you are currently running with, because you now have a family to take care of. Should the plan fail to bear fruit, that might badly affect family affairs. Gather as much information as possible, and move cautiously and with diligence. Make sure you have something to fall back on in case of speed humps along the way. Starting a new career at forty could be hazardous, but if you put your entire mind into it, with everything well planned out – well, you'll likely fall into the statistics of success, having made it after starting a completely new career at forty! Otherwise, it's always wonderful and wiser to grow or expand on what you already have at hand... what you've amassed over the years thus far.

WHAT IS YOUR AIM IN LIFE?
Do you want a job of natural security or a name for yourself? If you have some ability you are not utilising in your everyday occupation, get it out and give it a good dust. Look around and see if you cannot use it in your spare time or slot it into your social life segment. Lots of money can be made on the side.

YOU HAVE JUST LOST YOUR JOB
Why? Perhaps your qualifications did not fit in well. You did not perform to expected proficiency, or you simply lost interest in your job. Suffered burnout due to overwhelming workload, maybe? But that could be avoided by bringing it out to the responsible authorities; before it breaks you down... confide

in somebody for moral support. Perhaps you were just not interested in anything after something horrible happened. Anyway, now think carefully: were you doing what you can do best? If you were doing the best, this is the chance to even better yourself in the same field elsewhere. Do not, for goodness' sake, look back on this disappointment and let it colour your future moves. Tomorrow is always a far better day. If you were not doing what you can do best, now is your big chance to start all over again and wade in using your abilities to the best advantage.

Unemployed

Are your parents keeping you? Are you studying for something special? Were you born work-shy? What does it mean, 'not having a job'? Work is one of the greatest personality builders on the face of the earth. It builds character too. Character is the depth line of personality. If you are way off the route and do not want to work, time will hang on your hands sooner or later. You cannot rely on others forever. People will only be disposed to help if you're also trying hard from your end. A pleasing personality is liked by many people. It just feels right to invest in something that's productive – something that yields fruits or positive outcome – and not something that perpetuates idleness.

Buy a business or start one of your own, and that's even creating employment for others who are looking for jobs. Or you perhaps have difficulties in starting work? You must work because you need money to survive. Anyway, you could be really in need of getting a job. Back again to the old question: what can you do best? There is something you can do better than the next person – what is it? We are all born with distinct capabilities.

Write down everything. A devout paragraph can set you off onto a fresh line of thought. Be true and realistic to yourself. Now examine carefully all you can do. It may seem small and insignificant, but we all start from somewhere. What's left is to 'begin' the journey. Procrastinations or hesitations lead nowhere, and time won't stop ticking away.

Five Affirmations for Making You Feel You Are as Good as the Next Person

- I look good.
- I feel good and capable.
- I am strong, virile and adequate.
- I am emotionally stable.
- I am as good as the next person.

CHAPTER XI

UNPACKING THE INABILITY TO MOVE FORWARD

"I cannot go forward; so many things stop me." Many people might be scared for themselves, scared of their friends, or scared of their bosses, for instance, but they do go forward still – for as long as they carry on breathing, for every day that follows. They'll continue maturing age wise; get married, have children – divorce later on or sustain their marriages. Forward always – with no doubt.

But a forward march under the spell of fear is nerve-wracking. It makes so many things seem undesirable throughout your journey.

Are you afraid, or do you suffer from fear? Are your feelings afraid of being afraid? *Not sure if you can make sense of the question?* Can you not go forward because you fear what is around the corner?

Some individuals conceive themselves as temperamental and sensitive. Others blame their parents, relatives or other people as the reason of them failing to go forward. Some reasons could be legitimate, yes, but the negative notion can be overwritten with a logical pen of positivism. You are unique as an individual and have the power to formulate what you feel will be of benefit to you and others. Life is pretty short, but there's a lot to do in the given time. Fear cannot be allowed to muffle a glorious future you dream for yourself, and also contribute towards building a happy world you wish for others. Fear is a state of mind, and not going forward is an offshoot of this.

This is you and me, not only the other person. We need not be smug in it. We wake in the morning afraid to get up. Too cold! Afraid to eat breakfast – might be late for the office – or afraid to run for the train or bus. We fear traffic like an ominous monster, every day; yet in actual fact it won't be too bad after all. We fear what problems will arise during the day: miscalculations, mistakes, criticism. We're afraid to work a little bit late.

Are you afraid that you might miss the train home, afraid to open the front door, or afraid of what might have happened during your absence? Fire, accident, illness, burglary, infidelity? Must not eat too much for dinner, it might spoil our sleep. These and so many other fears torture us every single day, depleting our willpower. So, to bed we might go, dead tired. Dead tired *from what?* Is nervousness consuming a lot of energy and leaving you knackered – mentally and physically. Not on your life!

Are you exhausted by nervous fears and worries? Tomorrow you will not go forward at all because of being ruled by the old feelings of failure that belong to yesterday, digging up remembered emotions and expressions of the past. Nothing else so robs a man. Of course, you could have had failures in the past. No-one succeeds without at first having failed in most cases. Success is built upon a firm foundation of failure – failure recognised and rectified.

Inadequate control of emotions too can hinder progress in moving forward. Emotions control our actions. They control our sex urges, for instance. What we feel when we desire to possess a member of the opposite sex is an emotion. Sex begins with what we feel in our bodies and in our minds, but mostly in our minds; for sex motivation is controlled by thoughts. Sex would not be until and unless it's started. Many times, rape happens through hasty feelings and uncontrolled emotions. Should a child be conceived in such manner, it might not sound good to their ears when they get older and are told of their history – how they came about. It is crucial to control one's feelings! Wait for the appropriate time and it must be consensual. Respect the other party and by so doing you will be treating yourself with respect too.

One of the best ways to do this is to treat your body as if it were a real living thing or a temple – which it is, of course! But the body must be treated as if it had a mind of its own, as if almost every organ had a mind of its own with your brain being the main control centre. You need to send some messages to the other minds all over your body to put them in rightful functional order, to see and make sure the organs behave themselves well. That ensures your body performs healthily and is mentally fit. This is possible. It has been done and can be done by you too – by following the next affirmations or doing anything else similar, as circumstances dictate.

Dear Mind,

Alright, I will stop going around and around, trying to think four things at a time, sending some messages to my body like, I am ill, yes, I know... I worry too much... confused, I panic. Okay, I will relax... take it easy. As from today, I promise no more panic, just smooth, easy... relaxation.

Dear Heart,

Stop beating so fast. You are neither rheumatic nor tired nor weak but just a little bit anxious. I will breathe slowly, rhythmically. That's better. I know you always start pounding if I lose control over my breathing. When I am on the spot... or worried. From now on, I will consider you a bit more. I know you cannot take too much blood all at once. I will go easy on you; give you chance of controlled breathing... that is the secret.

Dear Stomach,

There I go again, making you ache! Making you really worry... guts! Amazing what you take from me. Unwholesome food pushed down into you at speed. Gastric juices reacting with vengeance. Wrong foods I take in at times. Tell you what, from today I'll embark on a proper diet, one gentle enough for you. I'll eat sensibly. I shall find out the perfect remedy to soothe you. I'll fast first and we'll get relieved for a time. I'll organise only good drinks for you, and we'll not fuss any longer. A good sleep is all we need for now. You shall soon get rid of those pains and ulcers. Nonsense, none of that for you anymore!

Dear Limbs,

Feeling shaky? You shake when asked to do so, that little extra... creak and creak first thing in the morning... it's all my fault... not exercising you enough, getting lazy! You are not what you used to be... Nonsense! You are as young as I let you feel. I promise to walk more, do a daily dozen, a bit of lifting, give you all some massage from time to time, stop sending out some toxins through negative thinking. Today, I will walk instead of riding. I will exercise in the fresh air. Today, I will sit upright, walk with my head up, chest out and stomach in. Today, my mind will be positive, my heart will be strong, my stomach will be settled, my arms and legs will feel free and light as air. I will breathe gently today. I will be calmer and cooler. I will collect my wits before I act.

In the case of anything gone amiss,
Take in a deep breath, slowly and calmly... feeling your chest filling up. Hold it for about ten seconds... and expel it mildly through the mouth, with a whooshing sound. Repeat the process, maybe three times. Think of each breath carefully; centre your mind around it. It is a very powerful tool to relieve anxiety. Now continue with your affirmations...

Today I will eat sensibly. I will eat slowly, and only process pleasant thoughts in the process.

Apply the positive suggestions to yourself today and every day.

The Conditioned Reflex

This is a set reaction to circumstances based on actions taken on other occasions or taught to us by experience in similar conditions, first discovered by Ivan Petrovich Pavlov, a physiologist in the early 1900s. A bang makes us jump. Why? Because a bang made us jump some time back. Such reflexes are built into the bodily system, and mostly do not call for conscious thought to take effect. We smell a sweet scent, and perhaps break a sweat or blush... why? Because that same scent reminds us of a romantic moment experienced some time ago. It could be a particular song or tune too that can trigger some memory. Someone says something to us we do not like and we may start to lose our tempers. Why? We lose our temper because something similar was said to us before.

Be careful not to overreact based on something negative that could have happened to you in the past. If a particular situation affected you to the core, do not be afraid to seek professional help. You'll be able to get through it with the right therapy. All you need is patience, allowing your body and mind to heal from the experience.

The Philosophy of Positivism – I am Personality

I was born without asking to be born. I was put into this world without my permission. Well, alright, so the world is mine. It asked for me, now it's got me. It has got to accept me and my ideas and my philosophy and allow me a chance to showcase what I'm capable of doing. The world owes me a living, a good one. I am going to work for it and get it. I know what I want in life. I will get all those people who are most likely to help me to get what I want right round me right now. I will hurt no-one in my endeavours. I will get what I want from life without injury to those with whom I associate, but I will still get what I want in life.

Philosophy of Negativism – I am Personality

Many people have made it out there. I didn't ask to be born, whatever dirty trick that my father and mother played in having me born. I don't see myself ever doing anything meaningful in a thousand, or millions of, years. What chances have I got of making a success out of my life? The world does not have to keep me if it does not want to, and surely it doesn't want to. I doubt anybody would want to know me personally out there, let alone listen to my problems. I will never get what I want out of life.

Of the above two, which one are you?

Positive means plus and negative means minus. Are *you* a plus personality or a minus personality? There is no-one who has had it easy all the time. You are unique, so always keep it in mind. There's absolutely no-one else like you. Gather all your courage and make the best out of your unique life. You are capable of good philosophy or pleasing character. Everyone's input in shaping the world is important, and counts. Turn your plaguing past into a vehicle that carries you over to a sunnier side, where the experiences become a story to share one day. Everybody starts from somewhere! Having passion is already a gift in its own right and shouldn't be undermined. It is a springboard that should action us to reach the next level.

You've Just Begun, but it Feels Like You're Suffering

Do not lose your grip. Suffering comes to most of us. Even if we have tonnes of money, we suffer sometimes. If we accept suffering, poverty, pain, shame, defeat, opposition and frustration, this can build a sturdy character. When we become philosophical (optimistic) about life, our character becomes softened. It makes it easier to handle tasks. There will be higher chances of us becoming more tolerant and beginning to understand others better, making it effortless to sympathise and possibly help out whichever way we can. We basically develop the capacity to feel for others. We think outwardly instead of thinking inwardly. We are no longer self-centred. In short, we appeal to others, we inspire them and we get them to share our outlook because we are willing to share theirs. That is the way to develop a positive philosophical personality. You give; you do not take away. You are plus, not minus. If you do not suffer, you are lucky, so try to be considerate towards those who really struggle: that is maturity, a stripe of honour.

How to Know What to Tell Yourself

You spend a lot of time telling yourself what to do. Sometimes, you talk out loud. Sometimes you tell yourself with your mind. The fact remains that a great deal of what you do every day is controlled and directed by what you tell yourself. However, it isn't always right or true. It's sometimes wrong, when negative. Your best friend in the world is yourself, though you do yourself wrong many times, perhaps – through bad auto-suggestion, and allowing bad hetero-suggestion to affect you. Auto-suggestion is what you tell yourself, as has been mentioned in other sections. Hetero-suggestion is what others tell you. Affirmations are things you affirm to yourself: it will, and it will be so. Auto-suggestion affirmations are tonic talks from you to yourself. They help to strengthen the mind.

Sample Tonic Talks

(a) I am going to be a great success at the match.
(b) I'll never feel any better in life.

Sample Reaction to (a)

You will exude confidence. It'll become easier getting both the mind and body ready to conquer.

Sample Reaction to (b)

Do not believe, you'll be just alright. Calling negativism to oneself is not good. It's not healthy to make this a habit. Some people ruin their lives by directing a stream of negative suggestions against themselves, either by accident or by design. Examples include... "I do foolish things over and over, what can people expect from me?" "I always look ill." "I feel faint always." "I'm likely to get terrible headaches." "I do not breathe properly every time I get onto the stage." "What is that pain now over my heart?" "My stomach will ache and that I know very well – I'll be sick!" "Oh, my legs will hurt if I walk down to the shops." "I know I will never ever make it in life." "I'll be the laughingstock of everyone." "Everything I lay my hand on flops!" "I will not get that job." "I'm going to forget all I have learnt come exam day." "With the first bite of the food I will start gassing, I know; I shall have to leave the party early." "I always feel so tired in the mornings." "I will never be able to wake up on time." "I'm bound to make a mistake." "I'm a failure, and *guess what?* It's my middle name."

What have I told myself here in Sample Reaction **(b)**?

I assured myself I will fail. I've equipped my mind and body for failure, which is neither good nor healthy at all. What you feed your mind with is usually dispensed accordingly.

REWRITE AS BELOW, ENCOURAGING INNER SELF

I feel fine, I look good, I feel strong, my stomach is settled, and I can breathe perfectly, no pains in my chest. Sickly? Impossible! I have no headaches; that's good. My legs feel perfect and ready to carry me around. I will make it. I will surely land that job. I shall remember all that I have learnt to date. I shall have fun today! I'll awake refreshed in the morning. I know I will eat one hell of a healthy meal. I will not make any silly mistakes – how could I possibly make mistakes when I really know what I am doing? I know I will succeed; I've been able to take everything in my stride. I have done exactly what people expected I would be able to do. I will never make any avoidable mistakes again. I am much better now, of course!

Now, create your own list of such tonic talks. Tell yourself and tell the world! Exercise them for self-assurance and confident living. Put them in your mental store for easy, quick reference – they should be repeated; it'll end up being the norm and will most likely keep you on the positive side.

I am confident and I am sure of myself. I can stand for myself and I speak well. I look good and feel completely great inside. I have personality. People like me and I interact with them well. Each day I get more confident and more purposeful. I have full control over myself.

The secret of successful tonic talks is to deny the subconscious of its wobbly suspicions that'll be inclined on the negative side and might hinder successful completion of targeted goals. Therefore, remember always to deny the obvious stress-triggering issues and conditions – be it in speaking, thinking, listening, watching, or personal actions. Halt consumption of sorrowful news, which might spike your anxiety levels unnecessarily – and leave you feeling hopeless and possibly sick.

AGAINST FEARFUL THOUGHTS

I fear nothing. Least of all do I fear being afraid. I know there is a reasonable sense of precaution, care and common sense. I see everything in its correct sense. I see everything in its correct perspective too and in rightful proportion. This being so, I have no need to fear. Fear is out-of-focus thought.

THINK, BREATHE, SLEEP BETTER

Since I think more clearly, my body is growing stronger. I feel stronger every day – I can feel the good blood flowing through my veins. I enjoy my control over my breathing. This means now I can control my thoughts, I can control my feelings, I no longer get upset and therefore I feel much stronger. I've been sleeping well and shall sleep well again tonight, and the next night.

DAILY DYNAMICS

Pick a week and try on this dynamic routine, or anything similar. It might possibly give you a mental bath.

Monday: Positive outlook from the time you wake up. Be an "I am all positive" personality. Storm your own way throughout the day and project yourself positively all the time, to everyone.

Tuesday: Get up early and do breathing exercises before jumping off the bed. Have a vitamin boost day! Organise foods that are high in antioxidants and vitamins A, B, C, D and E. Take a long walk before taking a bath and retiring to bed.

Wednesday: Today you can be a "yes man". Open up your mind. See what it feels like to say yes to everyone and everything small. Relax your mentality and allow others to help you out with hard tasks you have on your to-do list, because by now you have begun to develop a convincing and confident personality – and you're also beginning to believe in other people's capabilities too.

Thursday: A brisk walk before breakfast, about forty-five minutes. That will mean you'll get up extra early. Do not eat too much. Take another brisk walk later in the afternoon after the short, frugal noon meal. Have a healthy supper and indulge in a warm bath. Get a good cold rub afterwards and go to bed early.

Friday: Another day of being an "I am all positive" personality. Project yourself as you now know how to. Assure yourself, "I'm getting stronger each day, and I'm steadily conquering all my fears."

Saturday: Spend this day mingling as much as possible. Talking to another person can trigger good hormones that are helpful in fighting inner turmoil. Connect with family; it's soothing. Search for new friends if you feel the drive; you've been allowing positivity to flow freely within you from past days. Check around on remarkable things that have been done of late by popular figures, or your role models. Do something different! Today you must use a lot of physical and mental energy. Should you decide on going out to interact with others, leave good impressions behind you.

Sunday: Up from bed, soothe yourself with detox tea of choice. Rest today. Meditate. Take a good look into your immediate future. Plan with vision.

Most people are perfectly used to the expression that thoughts are real things. Many of us are convinced of the truth of this statement, yet few have a clear conception of what kind of a thing a thought-form is. Before we can understand the nature of thought forms, we must have some conception of the make-up of man and realise that he is not only the physical body with which we are all familiar. Man, the thinker, is clothed in a body composed of the subtle matter of the mental plane. Reality is only tangible when a thought is implemented into action. Set realistic plans for yourself and make sure you stay on the rightful path to realise them.

Give yourself several weeks on daily dynamics. Change routine from week to week to introduce novelty, both physically and mentally. Do not forget that popularity is the great reward of a pleasant and positive personality. It is a good sign of confidence as well. Get popular, at home, at work and amongst your close peers! Above all, reclaim your 'meant to be' cognitive legacy!

CHAPTER XII

INFORMATION ON GENERAL HEALTH AND SUCCESS IN JOB SEEKING

"The human body is a temple, and as such must be cared for and respected at all times" *The Hippocratic oath (circa 460-377 BC)*. What is put in the mouth has an impact on the body and its overall performance. The quality of life an individual leads is also dependent on what kind of foods the person consumes.

KEEP YOUR NUTRITIONAL INTAKE IN CHECK
To ensure a healthy lifestyle, it is always encouraged to observe the official Average Recommended Daily Dietary Allowance in relation to the stage of development, and not forsaking prescribed individual diets which might differ from person to person. Physical activity and exercising play a crucial role in the maintenance of a fit and flexible body. Drinking enough water is vital too, for normal wellbeing and sound functioning of the mind rather than just quenching thirst.

Water is a prerequisite for life. In an adult man, about 15 litres of water make up extra-cellular fluid; about 25 litres make up intra-cellular fluid; about 3 litres are present in the blood plasma, and 12 litres in the tissue fluid. About 60% of an adult body is water, according to Forbes, Cooper, and Mitchell (1953). Water is a major fluid solvent that is needed by the body to remove waste metabolic products and other toxins, mainly in the form of urea. Water is also important in the provision of a medium necessary for nutrients, enzymes and certain chemical substances to be fully diffused to allow the natural chemical body reactions to occur to sustain life. It is recommended to drink at least 2.5 litres of water on a regular day. This is the adult dosage, but is dependent on size, weather and bodily activities, amongst other factors.

Do Not Hurry or Rush Meals

Engage all your senses at mealtimes. Mindful and slow eating encourages one to chew food properly. It improves the digestive process, adding on to a slew of other important health benefits. The taste of food gets more pronounced too, and one will have a higher chance of appreciating flavours at a magnified degree. It is also good to avoid eating when in a temper, or when extremely exhausted. It might lead to undesirable effects such as binge eating, poor digestion or picking wrong foods altogether. All the factors count towards the general health of the body, including the state of mind.

Why Can't I be a Success in Life?

Are you permanently anxious about your health, imagining if you were like this or that, in one way or another? Do you dose yourself with pills and powders; drug away the earliest onset of pain without first trying to track down its source? Do you smoke excessively? Do you know that what you are doing could damage your body, but still have the 'who cares' mentality? Do you feel like it should always be another person doing good and right, and not necessarily you? Do you hesitate to accept responsibilities?

Is part of this a true picture of you? What do you intend doing about it all?

If you haven't started yet career-wise, or you feel you haven't really cracked it, take a moment and think carefully.

Contemplate. There could be lots of great potential in you right now. There might be the possibility of a masked skill or special ability that you never suspected you had. You are probably as fit as a fiddle, but only poisoning your blood stream with negative fear; simply afraid of getting started and easily giving in to that peculiar breathlessness; perhaps the one that usually catches up when venturing into something new. Allow the breathlessness to lean towards excitement, not fear. Giving in to the fear could be an indication that you are not convinced of yourself as a positive personality. Work on it. It's very possible to overcome.

Examine all the fields in which your special abilities might fit in. Choose one special sphere that falls closest to your heart. Develop your capabilities to fit into the requirements of that single sphere. Get to know people who have made it in that specific field. Visualise yourself as one of them, doing the job they do. Do not give up. Get your portfolio in place and ready. Reach out to them and sell yourself. This is also discussed in Chapter X.

You sometimes catch glimpses of people who seem to have accomplished a lot in life and perhaps wish you were like them. It all starts in the mind! Believe this; it is true. What you think about people, places and things comes right back at you in one way or another, and you get precisely whatever you give. Upon formulation of ideas, simply execute. Well, start by giving out positive thoughts about yourself. Let everyone know you are in rightful determination, and equally able. They'll catch on. Yes, they will catch on quickly enough if you stay real and stick to your purpose. The world is ready, waiting and open to receive your contributions. A lot needs to be done still. There could be much too that hasn't been discovered yet. The world can only be convinced by you. Go on and prove yourself!

WHAT DO YOU DO BEST?

When you were a child, you probably wanted to become a fireman, rock star, nurse, actor or any one of any number of options. Then, later on, growing into adolescence or late teens, ambitions could have changed or have somewhat matured into being more realistic in nature, according to your capabilities. It might well change later on in the years too, depending upon general life experiences and exposure.

The reason you are reading this book is probably that you are still in your late teens and might be perhaps still undecided, or you are already an adult but still haven't made the grade. Either way, you can still make it if you have the desire to. Always aim to make the best use of your abilities. There could be good chances of striking more opportunities to do and perhaps earn an extra something in addition to a normal day job.

Are you good at convincing people? That's a natural marketing skill that could be lying within. You could then become a broker, for example. Can you play an instrument? Can you draw exceptional pictures with your own hand? You could then become an illustrator, for example. Can you add up a column of figures with a flurry of figures? Look up the internet to see if you cannot find something along the lines that may allow you to work flexibly. The list is endless. Broaden your horizons. Search within yourself. Find out that talent that's in you. Go on and nurture it and let it blossom!

ARE YOU HAPPY IN YOUR JOB?

A good number of people complain of not being happy in their jobs, according to various research outcomes. They could be working just to get money. Wouldn't that be a despondent outlook, though? Wouldn't it be a waste of good life? Maybe you're not happy in your job because you're not quite convinced of your ability to carry out duties properly, or you perhaps lack adequate confidence in your future regarding your current position. In that case, there's a slim or no chance for growth, or you'll simply find it hard just getting by – day to day. Perhaps you have no confidence in your boss, or maybe you resent authority. You could be feeling very low too, amidst a string of other possible factors. Are you mixed up with rules and regulations? Is your work monotonous, unproductive, a dead-end job, underpaid, precarious, without a future, or too repetitive?

Quiz your stress ability state:
Do things hurt you easily? Is it difficult to remember detail? Does working in teams confuse you? Is there never enough time to do everything that's expected of you? Are you not following a healthy diet plan, and getting an adequate supply of all the necessary nutrients? Are your nights sleepless? How do you feel when you rise in the morning? Exhausted?

'Yes' responses to any or all the above questions might mean you are stressed. Some research sources suggest that stress is part of life, but only when manageable. Such stress can motivate one to work harder and improve things for the better. It should help you rise to meet challenges. If it leaves you frayed… oh, no! It is now working against your quality of life. Unbearable stress arises as much from one's discontent with one's job as from any other reasons (Strank, 2005).

"I cannot leave the job; it is the only thing for me to do."
"I won't get another job at my age." "There's too much competition; I can't risk making any changes."

This is a negative outlook. No-one should feel bonded. Were you not trained for anything other than what you're currently doing? Do you have nothing else at your fingertips? Why waste your time in such despondent resolutions? Why waste away your life in such a web of despair? Living from day to day in endless frustrations; longing for the work's siren to blow, or the office buzzer to buzz at the end of the day. Does something inside of you just not want you to get on? Have you spoken or aired your feelings to a trusted loved one? Nearly everyone has someone who is a source of inspiration. There is always someone who has placed his or her confidence in you, someone who expects you to make headway to be a success in life. Someone who would want to see you become the best version of yourself you possibly can be.

On Wanting to Change Your Job

You always find it difficult perhaps. Yes, you could indeed be frustrated and in need of more money, or other things. You might feel you'll be able to make more at some other place. First, be sure you can switch to another job right away or very soon after leaving your present occupation. Besides that, please love your job; you are taking someone's money each day! You ought to put your whole heart into what you are doing.

How to Land the Job You Want

You can spend months answering classified adverts or visiting employment agencies with no result. Now, learn to be your own job counsellor; learn how to research unlisted openings, write a forceful resume and perform smoothly in an interview. You can eventually transform a rejection into a job. You can be your own job counsellor if you put in vigorous effort into trying to get a job – and into keeping it when you get it. Cultivate an outgoing personality.

Follow these compiled rules developed by placement experts:

- *Find the hidden job market:* Classified adverts in local newspapers or any other newsletters may not reveal the wider range of openings. Widen your search criteria. Search the internet carefully and keep a list of reputable websites. Be vigilant of cyber scammers who at times take chances, preying on innocent job seekers. Not everybody is genuine at heart; always remember this. In as much as you might be desperate for a job, do not be gullible to every line that you read on the internet. Liaise also with some local agency; they usually have updated listings as well as elaborated information regarding specific jobs as well as the nature of companies. Write a very strong resume with a well-directed cover letter and send it to the relevant places. Vacancies might also happen within the company that you're currently working for. Keep developing yourself and sharpening your skills. Should there happen to be an opening at a more senior level, or just a particular department that you'll be aiming at... *why not grab the chance?* Go for it! Send your updated resume to the appropriate head within the company, specifying where you would like to work.
- *Locating hidden openings:* This step needs extra energy and determination to make telephone calls, for example, and consult with different people. Do thorough research and keep moving, despite rejections. Getting turned down should not affect your target goals. Contact anyone who

might possibly know of some openings, including relatives, friends, former teachers or lecturers, church members and individuals involved in community activities.

- *After finding a job opening:* Compose or re-adjust your resume accordingly, clearly highlighting the required crucial areas. Remember to stay true to what you're capable of doing and your actual level of training and experience. A resume is a self-advertisement which is designed to get you an opportunity for interview. Start by putting yourself in the place of the employer. Take stock of your job history and personal achievements. That might be useful from the employer's standpoint. Choose the most important ones and describe them in words that stress accomplishments. Avoid such phrases like "my work included... or my duties included". Use action words like planned, sold, trained and managed. Generally, it's unwise to mention salary requirements unless it's been requested. Write a convincing cover letter and send an original. While the resume may be just a copy, a covering letter must be personal.

IF YOU WANT PROMOTION

This is simple; all you need is courage. Send a letter to your superior or employer:

- Specify the number of years you have worked for the company.
- Mention the department you currently work in and your designation, and narrow down your reasons for wanting to move.
- Identify all you have learnt in your current position and clearly outline your readiness to move to the next level.

- Write down your qualifications, especially if you acquired something new after getting your current post.
- Explain your home circumstances if there's a need to do this.

Laws to Keep in Mind

If you can see a thing in your mind's eye, be assured there's a chance that you'll be able to get it. We all have a chance of being successful. When you think success, you can make it – just like money makes money. Think you are what you want to be, and you will be... a social success, for example, and you will become one. That which can be visualised can be realised. Positive thought is a confident thought. Determination and perseverance need to be allowed enough room in many cases, in order to make it in life, or to attain targeted goals. No mind should be so soft or pliable – like dough, or ductile like copper; that can be easily modelled to produce pretty bracelets to robust industrial machinery... that outside influences can completely rob it of its individuality: stripping it of its personality, or smothering its positive powers of progression. Hold fast to your integrity with honour.

CONCLUSION

There is nothing left to assemble. You have looked over your blueprint, checked everything in stock. You have taken all components, fitted them together and found out they make a great finished product. You have been working very hard to produce all this time. You have now made yourself a positive, purposeful personality and cultivated confidence and conviction. There remains the regular maintenance work to upkeep the brilliant functionality of the product. You must from time to time check over all you have learnt, polish up here and there. If and when you find spare parts are necessary, you have got an unlimited supply of them – church, support groups, mentors, other books too! Look carefully around you. This book can be your reference implement or tool to use in bolstering or carrying out running repairs, an additional item in your 'Do It Yourself' kit, for confidence and sound personality.

EPILOGUE

Once upon a time – in the Animal Kingdom, there was uncle Hare and his nephew, Baboon.

From a distance, one would easily confuse the relationship of Hare and Baboon as their being buddies. Hare and his nephew seemed very close indeed – always together, be it at shebeens, festivals or funerals. It all appeared hunky-dory and many admired them.

In reality, however, Hare, being the cleverer of the two, always wanted to benefit out of Baboon's slow thinking. He regarded his nephew as a pathetic decision maker. Hare surely outwitted Baboon in numerous scenarios and this added a spring to his step! Baboon never spilt any of his mishap encounters to the outside world. He snubbed the likelihood of being judged or made fun of by telling his story. He feared falling a victim of ridicule to many. There was never a moment for him to even sulk – onto his feet he quickly sprung back and kept going.

Baboon tolerated Hare's behaviour for a very, very long time, up until it reached a peak point and he made up in his mind that enough was enough.

Summer came, like all other previous years, but this time around it was welcomed with more zeal, marked by one of Hare's daughters, who got married. There was a lot of happiness in the village. Hare organised a huge bash to celebrate the momentous occurrence. He wanted the event to be the talk of the year or even beyond – big and spectacular! It was a send-off of his last daughter, who was also well-known for her mesmerising beauty. The news of the party travelled very fast throughout the village and it reached Baboon's ears too.

Baboon was an individual with a massive appetite for food. He salivated uncontrollably every time he heard anything to do with food. From the very moment he heard about Hare's organised bash he already saw himself as being responsible for the selection of perfect animals to slaughter. Slaughtering, he did not mind, but the job of skinning had to be reserved for others. He marvelled at the idea of him being the first volunteer to manage the barbecuing. The plan of roasting a whole goat made him drool and he wondered if he was going to get a satisfying portion of polenta to go with it.

"I just hope Hare doesn't play nasty tricks on me this time around. Oh, please..." Baboon quietly pleaded with the gods.

A smell of 'Kachasu' Traditional beer mischievously crept into his mind, and he wandered away.

The biggest calabash was placed in front of him. It was full to the brim and it had a thicker froth than any other brews ever before. All the other surrounding gourds were small.

The thought made him choke and he laughed out loudly. "Yeah, of course. I'm the oldest nephew and closest to Hare," he kept fantasising.

The rumbling noises emanating from his mouth startled his wife. Baboon's wife realised that the imagination of the father of her beautiful children – her beloved husband – had taken over. Baboon had turned into a zombie, holding a water vessel in his hands. She promptly poked him in his stomach, which was pulsating to the rhythm of his thoughts. He jumped, panicky, and spilt some water. They gazed at each other and both burst into laughter! The two began planning in unison.

They discussed all other previous events and how this one was likely to be the most special. They regarded themselves as the closest relatives to Hare's family. Baboon had also acted as the *go-between* during the dowry negotiations of the girl to be sent off. The two felt, with no doubt, that they would be given the utmost respect at the celebrations.

Everyone in the village, young and old, was eager to go to the celebrations but they were a bit sceptical of how Hare was going to treat the attendees. Hare was very stingy in his nature, not that he could not afford things, but out of pride. He would rather let any excess food in his house rot to trash than extend his arm. It was well known that he would literally prefer bugs and weevils to receive the food, over his fellow kinsmen. Showing off was his game. He would beg deliberately, out of mockery. Apparently, no-one ever internalised his kind of behaviour and they always hoped he would behave better at some time in the future.

A few days before the occasion, Hare's wife suggested to her husband that they keep their nephew Baboon out of the party. She never liked Baboon's odd eating habits and was afraid that he would eat most of the food at the festival, or even sneak some out to benefit his own family. Hare tried to persuade her and reminded his wife how Baboon had helped out with the go-between task, but Hare's wife was not buying any of it.

"This is my special daughter, my last born; won't I be allowed to make some of the decisions?" she declared to her husband.

Eventually, Hare thought of a cunning plan that would smartly keep Baboon and his family away.

Meanwhile, Baboon could not wait any longer for the big day to arrive. He sent his two older children to ask for salt at Hare's house so that they could spy on his behalf how the preparations were going. That was two days before the celebrations. The children were eager to go too. They went running!

Hare's in-laws had arrived and were getting royal treatment. The festival had literally begun in the eyes of Baboon's children. The smell of good food made them forget what they had been tasked by their parents to ask for. They were interrogated by Hare's wife, and non-meaningful responses came from both of them. One asked if Hare's cows were back in the kraal – having returned from grazing pastures – and the other simply mumbled with eyes wandering around. They were each given small pieces of meat to eat on their way back home.

"Alright... thanks for passing by. Now go before the sun sets!" Hare's wife insisted as she tried to quickly get rid of them – and off the youngsters went.

By evening time, the smell of barbecue had spread, stretching further into the village, and it reached Baboon's greedy nose. At dinner time he opted for carbs only. He ate a mountain of plain polenta with simply water on the side, to help get it down. He claimed that he could taste the divine meat that was being prepared at Hare's house in his mouth and did not want to spoil the glorious moment with the pumpkin leaves his wife had prepared.

The next day, very early in the morning, Hare went to Baboon's house to officially invite them. Baboon and his wife were in disbelief. They were overjoyed by the honour – it had been Hare himself, inviting them! The whole family danced all around and Baboon's wife ululated tirelessly.

Upon leaving, Hare left them with one crucial rule that was supposed to be obeyed by each and every person attending. Everybody was to be meticulously clean, including their paws.

"Cleanliness can never be much of a problem..." Baboon initially perceived and quickly agreed to adhere to the rule on the day. It did not ring bells to him how infeasible it would be. His family and himself were simply immersed in joy and overwhelmed by the gesture of an official invite. Nothing else could be of any better substance.

As soon as Hare arrived at his place, he started working on his 'dirty' project. He lit fire all around his homestead, burning the dry veld to ashes. His set up was such that the moment Baboon and his family walked into the yard on the big day, not just their paws would get dirty but their entire bodies too; from the dust of walking on ash. There were large flames rising very high into the sky and a thick smoke blanketed the whole village. The aftermath left soot and charcoal covering everywhere like carpet.

The big day arrived.

Hare's dream sadly came true. Baboon and his family found themselves filthy as soon they stepped onto Hare's territory. When they arrived at the doorstep, they were sent back to go and wash down at the river.

"We won't be long. Please reserve our seats!" Baboon promised Hare's assistants.

"Yes, we'll be back now-now," Baboon's wife assured them, cementing her husband's words.

The family ran as fast as their legs could carry them. Their active brood kept up with the pace too! Baboon targeted the nearest river and cascaded in the direction. In few minutes they had arrived.

Quickly, they washed. They scrubbed each other's backs and ducked into the cool river to rinse off. It did not take them much time, and soon after they dashed back enthusiastically. Their fur was clean and all shiny.

Upon return, they were told to check themselves. They were shocked, realising how soiled they were. They were ordered to go and clean up once more. Baboon and his family ambled back to the river. Their enthusiasm had plummeted. Food was already being served to other attendees. Little did they know they would be back and forth, back and forth to the river for the better part of the day. By the fifth time they were completely shattered. It was only later on, on the sixth occasion, that they realised it was the burnt veld that was making them dirty.

"Could we just be given food please. We'll sit at the gate," Baboon requested Hare's assistants. His voice was now frail. "Please – my kids are starving, I'm famished too," he pleaded.

Hare was told of the ordeal, but he was not in the mood to feel any sympathy. His project had worked out perfectly well. He stood up and went to face Baboon himself. "We've got to play a fair game, Nephew. Look, everybody inside here has stuck to the rules," he boasted. Immediately after, he left to do his host duties.

The ones who could fly had enjoyed their liberty to arrive immaculate, and those who could not had taken their time days before, to make body wrappings out of leaves and tree-bark. They had protected their paws and entire bodies. Wind could not sabotage their efforts either.

Baboon waited for a moment, stuck at the gate, but nobody seemed to be paying attention. He gave up eventually.

Leading his family, they all walked back home – hungry and extremely disappointed. It was the very first plot against Baboon that went public, and everybody got to know about it. It was the moment they learnt of the differences between Hare and his nephew, Baboon. It was an ultimate dismay to many.

Beyond the celebrations, Baboon and his uncle continued with their relationship, acting like nothing had happened. Hare assured him that it had been his own fault that his family had been denied entry to the special function; failure to stick to a simple rule they had all happily agreed on.

Baboon did not forget.

For the very first time, Baboon sat down with his family for a *serious* conversation. They perused all their previous numerous misfortunes. Baboon, as the head of the family, had to quickly learn and be in a position to psych his family on how they could move on and rescue themselves from the ugly reputation that had been set against their name. They all came up with an idea.

Baboon and his family organised their own huge celebrations. They sought help from their surrounding neighbours and other relatives. Help flourished from all the villagers at large. Baboon realised that they too in the village wanted to teach Hare a great lesson.

Everyone was invited to the feast, including Hare and his family, but Baboon also had a strict rule. The rule was publicised only two days before. It stipulated that food was only to be served and eaten up in the trees at a designated area. Hare and his family were not climbers, but they thought they would quickly learn on the day or ask good climbers to give them a hand to find their way up. They had already underestimated Baboon's intelligence.

The big day came, and most invitees arrived on time. They all climbed high up in the Marula tree as they each got there. All pots and calabashes were put high up too. Hare and his family had arrived early, like many. They exhausted all tricks to try and ascend but nothing worked in their favour.

Civet and his family turned up a little later than everyone else and Hare turned to him.

"Could you please go up with my young ones at least," he pleaded. Civet looked high up at the other villagers, who winked at him. "Sorry, Hare, I can't help. We have to stick to rules as always. Each individual is to climb up on their own," Civet highlighted emphatically, and up he and his family went, joining the others!

Hare's family just sat on the ground. They watched everyone else as they enjoyed themselves up in the Marula tree. They strained their heads looking up, thinking somebody would find it in their hearts to pity them, and would throw something down for them to at least get a bite. Alas – that hope never materialised.

The food smelt absolutely enticing. Only clean bones fell down from the massive tree. They watched as the bones kept dropping from all angles like hailstones, and they had to go and stand at a distance.

Who dares the strike of a heavy bone on their heads?

Hare looked at his family. He was not impressed at all. He saw immense sadness portrayed all over their faces. With silent good byes, they all turned their backs to walk away.

Disappointed, they strolled slowly and entered onto the track that led them home. Monkey, a very close friend of Baboon, screamed down at them that things go around like a wheel, and that days are never the same.

"Treat others the same way you also want them to treat you..." said Baboon, as he finally took it upon himself to give his uncle a lesson. He sang as he swung from one branch to another. They all kept shouting until Hare and his family were swallowed into the thicket and were completely out of sight.

Baboon and his allies partied till sunset, soaking up in immense merriment.

THE END

BIBLIOGRAPHY

Behr, A.L., Cherian, V.I., & Mwamwenda, T.S. (2013). An Educational Psychology for Schools in Africa, Butterworth-Heinemann

Bhattacherjee, A. (2012). Social Science Research: Principles, Methods, and Practices, 2nd edn, University of South Florida

Bowins, B. (2004). Psychological Defence Mechanisms: A New Perspective. *The American Journal of Psychoanalysis*, vol. 64, no. 1, pp. 1-26

Boyle. G.J., Matthews. G., & Saklofske, D. (2008). Personality Theories and Models: An Overview, Available online: https://www.researchgate.net/publication

Clark, D. & Gonza`lez, A.P. (2014). Obsessive-Compulsive Disorder, In P. Emmelkamp & T. Ehring (Eds), The Wiley Handbook of Anxiety Disorders, 1st edn, John Wiley & Sons

Deblec, J. & Ledoux, J. (2004). Fear and The Brain, *Social Research*, vol. 71, no. 4, pp. 807-818

Diehl, M., Hay, E., Chui, H., & Lumley, M.A. (2014). Change in Coping and Defence Mechanisms Across Adulthood: Longitudinal Findings in a European American Sample, *Developmental Psychology*, vol. 50, no. 20, pp. 634-648

Dwairy, M. (2002). Foundations of Psychological Dynamic Personality Theory of Collective People, *Clinical Psychology Review*, vol. 22, pp. 343-360

Feldman, R.S., & Garrison, M. (1993). Understanding Psychology, vol. 10, New York: McGraw-Hill

Forbes, R.M., Cooper, A.R., & Mitchell, H.H. (1953). The Composition of the Adult Human Body as Determined by Chemical Analysis, *Journal of Biological Chemistry*, vol. 203, no. 0021-9258, pp. 359-366, Available online: https://www.jbc.org/action/showPdf?pii=S0021-9258%2819%2952646-1 [Accessed 14th April 2021]

Gill, M.M. (1976). Metapsychology is Not Psychology, Psychological Issues

Haralambos, M., & Heald, R.M. (1980). Sociology Themes and Perspectives, 2nd edn, London: Bell and Heyman

Jager, W. (2003). Breaking 'Bad Habits': A Dynamic Perspective on Habit Formation and Change, Available online: https://www.researchgate.net/publication/

Johnson, E.J. (2010). Improving Positive Self-Confidence, Available online: https://www.researchgate.net/publications/

Kalat, J.W. (2021). Introduction to Psychology, Cengage Learning

Klockner, C.A., & Prugsmatz, S. (2012). Habits as Barriers to Changing Behavior, Available online: https://www.researchgate.net/publications/

Koch, S.E. (1959). Psychology: A Study of a Science

Lebohang, M. (2007). School Library Identity Card Processing System (Slicaps), Software Development Project, Department of Computer Science, National University of Science and Technology

Lebohang, M. (2020). Information Systems (IS) Governance and Sourcing, Strategic Management and Information Systems, Department of Informatics, Lund University

Lebohang, M. (2021a). Future of Education Case – Massive Open Online Courses (MOOCs), Designing Digitalisation, Department of Informatics, Lund University

Lebohang, M. (2021b). Is DevOps Digital Masters?, Designing Digitalisation, Lund Studies in Informatics – Student Paper, Department of Informatics, Lund University

Lebohang, M. (2021c). e-Learning in the Aftermath of the 2020 Pandemic: An Interpretive Analysis of Lund University Response, Master Thesis, Department of Informatics, Lund University

Lenin, I., et al. (1995). Adolescent Sexuality, AIDS Supplement, July edn

Maier, N.R.F. (1955). Psychology in Industry

Maldonaldo, J. & Spiegel, D. (2001). Conversion Disorder, Available online: https://www.researchgate.net/publication/

Manketlow, J. (2009). Building Your Self-Confidence, Available online: https://www.mindtools.com.pages/article/

Mwamwenda, T.S. (2020). Preface to the 4th edition Educational Psychology: An African Update Perspective, Ponte

Nyagura, L.M. (1993). Socio-Cultural Study for Population Education in Zimbabwe, An Unpublished Consultancy Report for UNESCO and Ministry of Education and Culture, Harare

Neckel, S. (1996). Inferiority: From Collective Status to Deficient Individuality, Social Review, Oxford: Blackwell Publishers

Pradhan, R.K. (2009). Character, Personality and Professionalism, *Social Science International*, vol. 25, no. 2, pp. 2-23

Schultz, D. P., & Schultz, S. E. (2017). Theories of Personality, 3rd edn, Boston: Cengage Learning

Rank, O. (1958). Beyond Psychology, vol. 485, Courier Corporation

Scrantino, A. (2018). Emotion, Stanford Encyclopedia of Philosophy, Available online: www.plato.edu

Solomon, R.C. (2004). Emotion, Available online: www.britannica.com/science/

Spearman, L. (2014). Inferiority Complex, USA: Trafford Publishers

Strank, J.W. (2005). Stress at Work: Management and Prevention, Amsterdam: Elsevier Publishing

Tapfuma, M., Xuelian, W., Mukundwa, D., Mollel, R.J., et al. (2021). COVID-19 Medical Student Perspective: Our Experience, European Journal of Pharmaceutical and Medical Research, vol. 8, no. 1, pp. 69-71, https://www.ejpmr.com/

Tapfuma, T.M. (2000). An Investigation of Problems Faced by School Heads and Teachers in the Teaching of HIV/AIDS Education in the Secondary Schools in Chinhoyi Urban Area of Mashonaland West Region, Research Project, Department of Pedagogics, Chinhoyi Technical Teachers College: University of Zimbabwe

Tashakkori, A., & Teddlie, C. (2010). SAGE Handbook of Mixed Methods in Social & Behavioural Research, 2nd edn, California: SAGE Publications, DOI: https://www.doi.org/10.4135/9781506335193

Vygotsky, L.S. (1972). The Psychology of Art

Woodworth, R.S. (1930). Dynamic Psychology

Zanamwe, L. (1995). Youth Sexuality and Reproductive Health: A Review of Literature and Youth Programmes in Zimbabwe Report on Behalf of ZNFPC

www.ingramcontent.com/pod-product-compliance
Lightning Source LLC
Chambersburg PA
CBHW022107160426
43198CB00008B/382